CITY SAFARI

WILDLIFE IN LONDON

Andrew Preater 6 B

CITY SAFARI
WILDLIFE IN LONDON

Gavin Weightman
Mike Birkhead

Sidgwick and Jackson
London
LWT

For William Morris Weightman, a great
naturalist, and Lucy and Ben who laugh at Lapwings,
and for Caroline 'Aitzey' Aitzetmuller

First published in Great Britain in 1986 by
Sidgwick & Jackson Limited

Designed by Ray Hyden
Produced by Baker Mahaffy Ltd
ISBN 0-283-99322-7 (hardcover)
ISBN 0-283-99323-5 (softcover)

Typeset by Type Generation Ltd
Printed and bound in Hong Kong by
Mandarin Offset Marketing (HK) Ltd
for Sidgwick & Jackson Limited
1 Tavistock Chambers, Bloomsbury Way
London WC1A 2SG

CONTENTS

The sun also rises over London, where a natural world exists in the concrete landscape of the city.

INTRODUCTION

THE WORD SAFARI means 'journey', and in the era of big game hunting in Africa it became a European term to describe the organised pursuit of elephants, lions and other large and fearsome creatures in some of the wildest country left in the world. To apply the same term to an exploration of wildlife in Bethnal Green or Belgravia, in which the hunter is armed with a street map, a field guide and a pair of binoculars, is to invite ridicule. So the title of this book and the television series it accompanies, is deliberately provocative. What we hope to provoke is not, of course, ridicule but a quite new and exciting vision of wildlife in one of the largest cities in the world, and an eagerness to study and explore the remarkable variety of creatures and plants that survive heroically and quite wild among seven million people.

Despite the great upsurge of interest in wildlife in recent years, encouraged by the natural history films on television and the emergence of ecology as a political issue, most people who live in towns remain blind to the natural world in their midst. They assume that if there were a great deal of wildlife about, they would notice it, and all they can really recall is the house sparrow, the pigeon and a story about the fox which chased someone's cat in Surbiton. It all sounds very tame, and quite unlike the wonderful world, full of colour and red in tooth and claw that they watched on television the other day: a safari in the African savannah, or South America or a tropical island.

The edited and distilled film vision of wildlife in remote regions gives quite a false impression of what it would be like for the untrained untutored visitor to go on safari in a region teeming with wildlife. He might see absolutely nothing at all, because he does not know where to look, or how to look for wild creatures. In the city, as anywhere else, you have to learn what to look for, and to explore.

For much of the time working on this book and the television series we have been in a small office on the twenty-second floor of a tower block overlooking the Thames, with St Paul's Cathedral to the east, and Parliament to the west. In the morning and evening rush hours, the bridges swarm with commuters heading to and from the main line railway stations south of the river. In their brisk walk across the bridge very few would notice or think to look for the birds we could see from the window: a heron flying over, mobbed by crows; flocks of black-headed gulls rising in thermals above the river as they gathered for the evening roost on one of London's reservoirs; the kestrel, which slid through the air by our window many times and hovered above the rooftops; skenes of cormorant in V-formation following the line of the river; the swarms of starlings silhouetted against a winter sunset above Trafalgar Square; the occasional winter flocks of lapwings with their bouncing flight as if each were suspended on a rubber string; the geese and wild duck flying stiff-winged, in clockwork motion against a backdrop of Embankment offices. When we pointed out these sights to others working in the same building we were often given incredulous looks, as if the effort of searching for wildlife in town had driven us mad, and we were hallucinating.

Many times this sedentary, desk-bound observation from our giant concrete hide in the heart of London interrupted our research and the planning of trips to the wilder and more inaccessible parts of the capital. In the East End of London, in particular, we were taken to some very strange places. Our guide would lead us to a desolate road near Barking Creek, where the winter wind cut across overgrown land-fill rubbish tips, abandoned power stations and stinking chemical factories. Then we would follow through a gap in a wire fence into a kind of savannah of wasteland plants and self-seeded elder, buddleia and birch trees.

In the snow, we would see the tracks of rabbits and foxes. A wheeling flock of several hundred linnets, beautiful little birds when seen magnified through binoculars, would rise from the scrubby plants. We would hear that the bird trappers who once took these birds in their hundreds before the laws protecting such species came in were at work again, with their mist nests and traps. With a clatter, partridge would fly up from their hiding place below a piece of rusted machinery.

Over several months our exploration took us to Buckingham Palace Garden, reservoirs, canals, railway sidings, Heathrow airport, sewage works, in a landrover across the almost Scottish landscape of Richmond Park, dazzling hay-meadows near Cockfosters and an ancient wood near the Hoover Factory building in west London. In a landrover we bounced over acres of rubbish tips to watch the catching and ringing of migratory seagulls which thrive on the capital's debris each winter, many travelling all the way from the Baltic.

There is a romantic notion, shared by naturalists and laymen alike, that wildlife has the same sensibilities about landscape as man, and 'prefers' to be in the countryside, which looks and feels more natural, than the town. If you imagine that wildlife needs and seeks out attractive rural scenery, then, of course, you do not expect to see it in London or other cities. But wildlife has no inclination to contemplate the beauties of nature: its needs are more immediate and it will go anywhere, even to the ugliest places, if there is food and the right conditions for it to breed. Those conditions can be fulfilled in the most unlikely ways, and however man re-arranges the component parts of the landscape there is some wildlife which will be able to exploit it.

This is just as well, for there is hardly an acre of ground in Britain and precious little in Europe, which is not man-made in the sense that the primeval vegetation has been removed, up-rooted, replanted and replaced by centuries of farming, felling of trees and tending of domestic animals. The wildlife which survived this transformation of the landscape had to make do with conditions quite unlike those in which its ancestors evolved, and managed to do so long before towns were built.

We found that for many people, the term 'wildlife' meant large, fierce beasts like lions, and that it was almost laughable to apply it to the much smaller and less threatening creatures that could be found in town. But there does not seem to be any good reason why the term 'wildlife' – probably an American import of the 1940s – should be reserved for the biggest, fiercest of zoo animals. If it were, there would be virtually no wildlife in Britain.

A recognition that urban wildlife can be treated in the same way as the more exotic creatures of wilder regions of the world is our final justification for calling our exploration *City Safari*. We will encounter some quite rare plants and birds, follow some fascinating historical trails, and by the end of it we hope provide a convincing argument that our enterprise was not far-fetched.

We have given an account of some of the problems we had in capturing urban wildlife on film, and these should give an idea of why it is necessary to carefully track and observe wildlife in town if all the secrets of the city are to be revealed. One of our first visits was to London Zoo itself, for here we hoped to find the wildlife of the capital living freely alongside the elephants, giraffes and lions captured on safari in Africa.

The mallard, one of the most beautiful wild birds in London.

Just across Regent's Park from London Zoo is a heronry, where young herons have a tree-top view of Baker Street and the Abbey National Building Society offices.

UNTAMED LONDON

YOU WOULD IMAGINE observing wildlife, recording its behaviour, and filming it to be a very peaceful kind of occupation; quite often it is, because absolutely nothing happens. Then, suddenly, a drama unfolds and is over in a few seconds – and you have missed it. This happened over and over again in our exploration of London's wildlife and induced a kind of tension and nervousness which was quite unexpected. Nature-watching can be a very stressful business if you are trying to understand and record what is going on.

It had become a tedious jibe that the only place in London we would find any wildlife was in the capital's famous zoo, opened in 1828 in Regent's Park, and now thirty-four acres of cages and enclosures holding more than 1,000 species from all over the world. And it is true that when you arrive in Regent's Park early in the morning there is a quite extraordinary cacophony of wild-life sounds echoing from the regency terraces around the park, rather like the soundtrack for *Tarzan of the Apes*. Gibbons, those very athletic monkeys, make jungle-like whooping sounds, parrots screech as if infuriated by what one of them has just said, and there are cackles, moans and groans which say instantly: 'wildlife'. Somehow, the dawn chorus of London blackbirds, thrushes, dunnocks, robins, wrens, crows and sparrows does not have the same exciting effect.

However, the Zoo turned out to be the perfect place to show London's wildlife alongside the zoo animals. Though the exotic collection of lions, tigers, elephants, and rhinos provided a vivid illustration of the wildlife that is not at large in the city, in, around and amongst them were truly wild creatures which make up a kind of free-range zoo in their own right. There were grey herons flying in to steal fish from the sea-lions, flocks of herring and black-headed gulls pestering the penguins, as well as grey squirrels, crows, magpies, greenfinches, and rabbits. Some of the zoo keepers take an interest in this uncaged wildlife, and told us of foxes, hedgehogs, owls, stag beetles and one heroic little bird – the moorhen.

Moorhens are rather like small black chickens with a red patch on their forehead. They are very common in the parks of the city, wherever there is water, and for them the zoo with its ponds and plenty of food is as good a place to establish a territory as any-where else. But we could hardly believe our luck when we learned that it was an established tradition in the zoo that a pair of these birds would nest in the lion enclosure. This is an ideal spot for them because the new lion terraces are not enclosed by wire or walls on all sides. The king of beasts is hemmed in by a deep pond which forms a security moat. Moorhens are aquatic birds and build their nests on or near the water, so the lion enclosure provides them with all they need.

In the spring, we waited to see if the moorhens would oblige us by nesting next to the lions. And they did, though

The true wildlife of London under the nose of a lion in London Zoo: the moorhen hunts fish in the lions' pool and nests here.

to our disappointment you could not really see the nest, which was hidden by a creeping plant and tucked away in a corner; and was only approachable with a camera if you risked your life by climbing in amongst the lions. Obviously, visitors to the zoo had noticed this small bird which was apparently taking a chance by swimming around in such a dangerous place, for there is a notice which reassures everyone that lions are not interested in eating moorhens, although both lions and tigers have been known to capture and eat mallard duck. It also says that the fish which can be seen swimming around in the lions' pool are especially safe, because the grey herons which visit the zoo dare not land there.

Armed with this information, we set up to film the moorhens. We watched them feeding their chicks on the lake, and one bird made an occasional sortie to a litter-bin which it fell into in a comical fashion. This was all very well, but we had great difficulty getting any shots showing the moorhens close to the lions. Most of the time, the lions yawned, slept, groomed, slept, yawned and stared, while the moorhens trotted busily around pecking at invisible snippets of food, tiny grubs and insects on which they feed their young.

If a lion stood up there was immense excitement at the thought that it was all about to happen: an interaction between the king of beasts and one of London's truly wild creatures. Then the lion would turn round, like a dog in its basket, and go back to sleep. We were once startled by a lion's roar, but it came from a machine in which you put ten pence to get a commentary on the lions from Johnny Morris. Our attention strayed from the moorhens to the sparrows which hop along the scenic logs in the enclosure and preen themselves within inches of the lions. Other birds were nesting in the shrubs around the enclosure. A blackbird col-

lected beakfuls of grass by the pool, and mud to cement it into a nest on the edge of the lion enclosure. And one day a mallard duck arrived with a brood of chicks which she led around the pool and along the shore, with a good deal of quacking as a mallard drake was pestering her. All this went on in the lion enclosure.

It was pleasing to watch this activity, and encouraging in that here we had very clear proof that the captive zoo animals were not the only wildlife that could be found in the city. But there was always a nagging feeling that a moorhen or a mallard duck would not be accepted as *wildlife;* they were just scavengers which fed from litter-bins and, from bread in the park or on bird tables. After all, how could these birds be wild if they lived in a town and were not frightened of man? Surely this was unnatural, and the interesting bits of behaviour that so enliven studies of wild creatures would be absent in these urban creatures.

We knew from our research that urban species behave in very much the same way as their rural relatives, and that a moorhen in the zoo is like a moorhen anywhere else whether in the town or in the country. And there was a particular piece of behaviour for which we were looking. Moorhens usually have two broods of chicks, and the first brood, before they leave their parents, help to patch up the nest and to feed the second brood. It is a piece of altruistic behaviour which is found in a number of British species like house martins, long-tailed tits and dunnocks, and has been the centre of much argument amongst evolutionary theorists because all individual animals are supposed to be intrinsically selfish, and a young moorhen clearly is not.

We were told by the zoo keepers that the moorhens in the lion enclosure had often been seen with two broods, the first helping to raise the second. But for this to happen the first brood has to survive, and we were not fully prepared for what happened next. One day we were filming the lions on the end of a telescopic lens because we wanted a shot of them 'appearing to roar' – there was no hope of the real thing, but a yawn with the right soundtrack super-imposed would do. The moorhens were busy as usual, one parent on the pool with a couple of chicks, and the lions were characteristically unhelpful. Sud-denly, a flash of white wings appeared, the cameraman looked up, swung around and tried in vain to focus on the moorhen. We stared as a herring gull swooped down, picked a moorhen chick up in its beak and flew off with this pathetic ball of black feathers half-swallowed. It was then we realised that there was now only one chick left, and the sequence of one brood feeding another was probably not going to be possible that year.

There were some other surprises in the lion enclosure. Though the notice says that the fish in the pool are safe from herons, it does not say that they are caught by the moorhens. On several occasions we saw the bird peck a live fish from the water and hammer it into insensibility, while the lions appeared to observe this miniature hunting scene with disdain. There was also a fearful

A moorhen feeding its chicks on the pool in the lion enclosure: tiny insects are essential for the young birds, which themselves often become a meal for herring gulls which nest in the zoo.

Grey squirrels in the London parks have become almost like pets, but they are wild, and do not survive entirely on food scavenged from man.

territorial battle on the pool when the mallard duck, worried by the drake, took her brood too near the moorhens. Like two 'men o'war' the moorhens attacked the mallard and drove her off.

It was beyond doubt that these birds were wild: they were hunting, fishing, fighting for territory and behaving as they would in the countryside.

One of the other creatures in the zoo was the grey squirrel, which many Londoners regard either as a pet or a pest. We had often seen them popping in and out of wastebins, but of course they would not do this when we were filming them. So we resorted to the established procedure of wildlife film-makers and tried to encourage the squirrel to do what we wanted. With some salted peanuts one was enticed down from a tree, and, about ten packets of peanuts later, into a litter bin. It then sat engagingly on a wall and would not perform again because a passer-by, unaware that a serious natural history film was in production, gave it a packet of potato crisps. We were about to abandon the squirrel when a magpie appeared.

There are plenty of magpies in the zoo, and several pairs nest there, but they are not easy to approach. However, this particular magpie could not resist the enormous supply of salted peanuts that had been scattered to induce the grey squirrel, now tucking into potato crisps, down from the tree. Magpies are very beautiful birds, and though they appear to be simply black and white from a distance, there is an iridescent blue in the feathers on their back. With their long flicking tails they look almost tropical.

A number of animals when faced with a surfeit of food will collect and store it (referred to as 'caching' by zoologists). This is what the magpie began to do, gobbling up one peanut after another until its crop was full, then hopping off to disgorge the load

into a hole in the ground – at a discrete distance, and behind a tree so that we got a memorable shot of a magpie just out of sight.

Then the squirrel, which had finished its crisps, began to collect nuts. We watched it gather two or three in its mouth, then scamper around in a rather thoughtful way to a spot where it too dug a hole, dropped the nuts in, pushed them down with its snout and covered them over with its paws. The magpie then stopped collecting for itself, and sat in a low branch watching the squirrel. As soon as the squirrel had finished burying the nuts and gone off to find some more for its larder, the magpie hopped down and dug up what the squirrel had just buried. This went on for some time, before the squirrel chased the magpie away. We saw the same thing happen in Hyde Park with the carrion crows. An old lady was seen walking up the Broadwalk with a group of three or four squirrels tagging along behind. She fed the squirrels with peanuts and they in turn went to bury the nuts only to have them stolen by the crows.

This fable of the squirrel and the magpie was a bit of wild behaviour that we were fortunate enough to watch and film, and we began to realise that the town provided opportunities for cameraman that the countryside could not because the animals would be so much harder to approach. Urban wildlife would perform naturally but unselfconsciously in the most public of places.

There was no doubt that this London wildlife behaved in a way which was every bit as interesting as rural wildlife, but there was still the intriguing question of how it survived in town. Could grey squirrels, for example, live entirely on potato crisps, and could magpies live on peanuts? Wildlife in towns is often dismissed as a 'bunch of scavengers' as if the fact that it relied on 'unnatural foods' somehow destroyed

its claim to be wildlife at all.

We puzzled over this a great deal, and tried to work out how the city ecosystem worked, and how it differed from more natural ecosystems in the countryside. In the textbook model of an ecosystem, all life is based on green plants; without them, practically nothing can survive. It is green plants which, through a process of photosynthesis, manufacture sugar from water and carbon dioxide with the energy provided by sunlight. All other creatures in the ecosystem get their energy either from eating plants, or eating things which eat plants. At the top of the food chain are those creatures that are not eaten themselves.

Scavenging, which is really eating the left-overs from someone else's meal, is very much part of the textbook ecosystem and goes on in the countryside and the wildest parts of the world. Vultures, for example, live by scavenging the carcasses of dead animals, and there is always a fair amount of

Though such perfectly manicured landscapes as this in Regent's Park are no use to some kinds of wildlife, the green plants do provide the basis of a natural ecosystem.

waste material around to be eaten by animals like hyenas. So scavenging is not an entirely 'unnatural' way of getting food in the wild, and it is common in the countryside where foxes will raid chicken sheds and birds will eat grain sown in the fields.

In towns, however, there is far more food around to be scavenged than in the countryside, because so much waste is scattered about by the people that live there. Although all this food, whether it is crisps or peanuts, has been created by a natural ecosystem operating somewhere, it is delivered to the wildlife in towns in artificial abundance, and those creatures that can eat it will do very well indeed. But that does not mean that the *only* food for wildlife in towns comes from a rubbish-tip type of ecosystem, and that green plants are of no importance at all.

Just imagine, for a moment, what could survive in the city if there were absolutely no trees or plants at all, and if the only food available was human left-overs of one sort or another. The answer is, probably, not a great deal. Take, for example, grey herons; if they had an ample supply of fish from the zoo they would just about manage, but the sea-lion pool could hardly provide enough food to supply all the herons in London. They hunt fish and frogs all over the capital, and most of what they eat is ultimately dependent on the green plants that grow in London. A critical time of year for all species is the early summer when the young are being fed. Most fledgling birds need a high protein diet which can only be provided by insects. Even house sparrows, which often appear to be scavengers, can be seen hunting butterflies and caterpillars in parks and gardens to feed their young.

The only birds we could think of which might get by in a city without any green plants at all were the pigeons. Along with very few other species of bird, emperor penguins and greater flamingoes, the pigeon can make a kind of 'milk' which it feeds to its young for the first two weeks after they are born. It is not quite the same as the milk produced by the mammary glands of mammals. Pigeon's milk is made by both the male and female birds in the crop, where food is normally stored. It enables the birds to turn all kinds of scraps, from pop corn to Kentucky Fried chicken, into a white liquid, rich in fat and protein.

It may well be that this very unusual ability of the pigeon is the reason it is so successful in the rockiest parts of town, where little natural food is available. London pigeons do, however, eat quite a lot of natural food in the city, going to wasteground for weed seeds and eating berries in the parks. Woodpigeons, which are very common in London, also produce milk but do less scavenging.

All mammals produce milk, and so in theory should be able to convert junk food into something that they can feed to their young. But it is unlikely that foxes or hedgehogs would do very well in town if they lived entirely from food from rubbish bins or saucers of milk. Some research on London foxes suggests that they find only a third of their food by scavenging, and the rest is fruit, insects and other animals, all of which are dependent on green plants in the city. In other towns, such as Bristol, scavenging is more important for foxes.

So a city without any green plants at all would be very poor in wildlife. Possibly the brown rat, cockroaches, and the house mouse would continue to do well, along with the pigeon and a few sparrows. There might be clothes moths – although these have suffered since the introduction of synthetic materials which their larvae cannot eat – some kinds of scavenging ant and other insects, and spiders which live on those insects. It might be possible too

Many people mistake the free flying herons which steal fish from the sea lions in London Zoo for birds escaped from captivity – but this grey heron is wild.

for a predator right at the top of the food chain to feed on, say, a pigeon lower down which in turn has survived entirely on scavenged food. In towns, kestrels eat sparrows, which scavenge for much of their food. But it is difficult to imagine very much of a food chain, even in towns, without plants.

As there is more scavenging in towns than in the countryside, a few species which can thrive on the rubbish-tip ecosystem do exceptionally well, and very often are regarded as pests, but wildlife in cities is more dependent on what vegetation can be found there than is often realised.

Very little of the greenery that can be found in towns actually looks like that found in the countryside, and for that reason is often thought to be no good for wildlife. But our countryside is not at all natural: it has been transformed by centuries of agriculture that have turned woodland into pasture, hedgerows and ploughed fields. Even old woodland was managed, with the trees coppiced and pollarded, and felled for timber. What wildlife there is in Britain has to contend with this extensive alteration of the landscape which began long before cities were built. And managed vegetation 'works' in exactly the same way as wild plants in terms of photosynthesis; what has changed is the relationship between all the bits of the ecosystem, not the basis of its energy.

There is, within London and all large cities, a great deal of greenery, in parks and gardens, playing-fields, woods and wasteground. There is also plenty of fresh water in the canals, park ponds and reservoirs. On this vegetation, whether on land or in water, live a large number of insects which are eaten by birds and mammals, and by each other. In this sense, there is a natural world at work in the city, just as there is in the countryside.

You will generally find a greater

range of wildlife in the countryside than in the town, but suburbia, with its acres of gardens and low density of housing, compares pretty well with many tracts of farming land, and may be richer in some wildlife than the more mechanised, agricultural farming areas. What makes the difference is the amount and range of vegetation that can be found there. This might appear to be a very elaborate statement of a simple point, but it is important to understand the degree to which wildlife in towns is not simply an odd collection of half-tame scavenging animals, but is dependent on the ecosystem and food chains that are normally associated only with the countryside.

Within the built-up area of London,

Though house sparrows scavenge food from man they provide a natural food for the kestrel, turning popcorn into protein in the peculiar ecosystem of the city.

A mistle thrush with a worm in Regent's Park.

there are about sixty species of breeding bird, about twenty mammals, amphibians (such as the frog and newt), reptiles (such as the grass snake and common lizard), more than one hundred species of fish in the River Thames, more than sixty species of spider in Buckingham Palace Garden alone, and many insects including moths and butterflies that are restricted to particular food plants needed by their caterpillars. Most of this wildlife in the city is dependent on the scattered and often manicured vegetation of its parks and gardens, on its canals, lakes and the River Thames.

The natural resources available in the city are important not only for the food they provide, but for nesting material, places to hide and places to shelter. Most birds nest in trees, and need grass and twigs and mud for building materials. Those which nest in holes or under the eaves of roofs also need natural materials to construct and line their nests. You will see bits of plastic and string in the nests of blackbirds or coots, but it is rare for birds to build entirely from synthetic materials. And all wildlife make use to some extent of the products of the city's natural resources. As everyone knows, blackbirds and thrushes eat worms which they pull from lawns and flowerbeds. Starlings can be seen in the parks prising the grass roots apart with their beaks to find all kinds of insects. Any piece of turf which is not killed by fertilisers or insecticides is like a miniature jungle when put under the microscope.

Many species have a mixed diet, partly provided by the natural system, and partly made up by the 'rubbish-tip' system. But we wondered how many species there were which *never* scavenged at all and depended entirely for their food on the natural ecosystem. In the last few years, the records of the London Natural History Society told us, a bird called the house martin had established a colony right in the centre of London, close to Hyde Park, one of the largest open spaces in London, with a lake and mature trees, bordered by Park Lane and surrounded by fashionable Knightsbridge, Kensington and Bayswater. These small, dark blue, white-bellied birds, which fly like tiny jet aeroplanes, feed only on what is called aerial plankton – masses of tiny insects which float up into the air from water and plants, greenfly, and young spiders which 'balloon' on slender threads into the sky. Nobody feeds bread or peanuts to a house martin. The martin is a migratory bird which, spends the winter in Africa, south of the Sahara, as does its close relative the swallow, and the swift which it resembles. Each year martins travel thousands of miles to Europe, crossing the Sahara desert to breed. One explanation for this mysterious behaviour is that the North European summer provides a great abundance of flies and midges and this, together with the long summer days, means that they can rear more offspring than if they stayed in Africa.

At the start of the spring, when we were due to film the house martins, it seemed that they were not very numerous. The spread of the desert in Northern Africa has made the migratory trip of many birds more hazardous. We knew where the martins had nested before in Knightsbridge, and went down to look at the earliest possible date – but saw nothing. Then, a few days later, there they were wheeling around the Sheraton Tower Hotel, and dipping under the stucco eaves of the French embassy. It was an exhilarating sight, spoiled only by the fact that peering at the French embassy with binoculars brought some enquiries from the local police.

Not long after, we saw swallows flying over the Serpentine lake in Hyde

House martins, summer migrants from Africa, collecting mud for their Belgravia nests from pools by the Serpentine: a perfect example of wildlife moulding the natural world into the fabric of the city.

Park, and then one morning there were dozens of swifts hawking insects above the water. It was not going to be such a bad year after all, and we could begin to film the house martins – wildlife which was definitely not dependent on the rubbish-tip ecosystem.

Filming these birds was not easy because they fly so fast – rather like playing a game of space invaders where the problem is how to keep the bird in sight and in focus. But, when captured in slow motion, the martins, swifts and swallows look very beautiful. We had been told where the house martins usually took the mud for their nests, which they collect on the ground using their beaks as a kind of trowel. We were lucky enough to film this at one end of the Serpentine, right next to a café,

where some puddles had formed after the rain. It was more difficult to get film of their nests, for these were hidden away in the stucco rosettes under the eaves of the French embassy and the building opposite, with a set of four tucked into each rosette. House martins nest in many places in London and other cities, and, as their name implies, are at home in the city and probably have been for several thousand years, though their natural nesting place is on cliffs.

On many occasions there were more swifts to be seen over the Serpentine than house martins, though, as far as we know, swifts do not nest immediately around the park. They are well established in the inner suburbs and form flocks which screech around the

Swifts feeding over the Serpentine: these birds never scavenge from man.

rooftops in mid-summer. Swifts build their shallow cup-shaped nests out of sight under the eaves of houses using mud, grass and feathers cemented together with spit. Swallows build inside buildings not outside, and martins characteristically cement their nests to the sides of buildings. For this reason it is easier to spot martins' nests from the street.

Distinguishing these birds in flight takes a bit of practice, as often the difference in colour – the brown of the swift, and the blue and white of the swallows and martins – does not show. It is the shape which is critical – the silhouette which all field guides show. It is probably the availability of suitable nesting-places rather than food supply which restricts the breeding of swallows to outer London, but they can sometimes be seen in the centre, par-ticularly during spring and autumn on migration.

To find nests to film we set up a network of informers, members of the London Natural History Society and keen 'birders' – as bird watchers call themselves – to keep a look out. There was one species we were keen to find nesting in Hyde Park, because it is becoming much more common in London; it lives entirely on insects and builds a very attractive nest. This was the long-tailed tit, a pretty little bird with a small black and white body, and as its name implies, a long tail. It is quite secretive, though the insistent twittering of a flock sometimes gives them away.

In the previous year, two nests had been found in Hyde Park, and we were anxious to find one being built. The long-tailed tit takes a long time over its nest, constructing it from spiders' webs, grass and feathers, and decorating it with lichen, producing a domed structure with a small hole in the side. One of our contacts had once seen them use tissue paper as a substitute for lichen. We were, however, unlucky – the birds were there but we did not find the nest. Later we learned that five pairs of these birds had nested in Battersea Park and we had missed them. But, thanks to the keen observation of a gardener in Richmond Park we were able to film nest-building there, and later some scenes with the parent birds feeding their young.

Another species we were very lucky to film was a bird which was once an endangered species, and is now well established in London and other towns. This is the great crested grebe, a diving bird the size of a large duck, but more elegant and slimmer in shape. It has the sort of joke name that has non-naturalists guffawing. The grebe lives on fish, which it catches under water, and it does well on the Serpentine, which is well stocked with food of about the right size. There is a problem filming the birds hunting, because you can follow them until they dive, but you have no idea where they will emerge. However, on several occasions we were able to record grebes with fish in their beaks. More than one pair of grebes nested in Hyde Park, and it was possible to get close to them without a hide. When the chicks hatch, the parent birds fish much more frequently to provide them with food, and it was one of our most remarkable experiences to stand on the edge of the Serpentine, with passers-by wondering what had attracted our interest, while the grebes fed their young.

Birds provide the wildlife film maker with his easiest 'prey', and we were conscious that this distorted the picture of what there was in the centre of London. So we thought we should try for some other kinds of animal which had a diet of natural foods and could not be described as scavengers. There were hedgehogs, which are dependent on small grubs and worms for their food, but these are so familiar to many people who put out milk for them that we thought the image was not right. Much better would be a sequence showing bats in Hyde Park. We knew they were there because roosting bats were often found when a dangerous tree was felled in the park, and the Flora and Fauna Preservation Society had just started to put up 'bat boxes' to replace the lost roosting-places of these flying mammals.

Like the house martins, bats feed on insects which they catch on the wing, the type and size of insect depending on the species of bat. But the problem is, of course, that bats are nocturnal, and filming a small creature zapping around a darkened sky is almost impossible.

Undaunted, we met up one evening with two bat-watchers from the Flora and Fauna Preservation Society, and waited for the sun to go down and the gas lamps to come on in the park, to provide the right kind of spooky twilight for a short interview. This was at the Dell end of the Serpentine – where, the park police had told us, bats often emerged at night. Our two experts (nicknamed inevitably Batman and Robin) were armed with small bat detectors, which look rather like 1960s transistor radios and are designed to pick up the high-pitched sounds bats emit when hunting. Each species of bat has its own frequency, so the detector can identify particular species of bats.

We were prepared for a fruitless evening as the bat-watchers themselves were not too hopeful. It was early in the year for bats to emerge, and, as people politically committed to the idea that parks are not properly managed on behalf of bats – there should be more

dead trees and long grass – the bat-watchers seemed almost reluctant to admit that there could be many there.

When the gas lamps came on, joggers went by in the deepening gloom like panting, luminous phantoms, and we filmed the batmen wandering about aimlessly with their little trannies like a couple of lost souls from the 1960s. Anything that flew overhead and caught the eye brought a cry of 'Look!', and we would get a glimpse of a mallard duck gliding on to the Serpentine. Then, just before night began to fall, we saw a bat. The bat detectors began to emit a thrilling, repeated signal, a kind of 'mouse code' which crackled, and our batmen said in unison: 'Noctule . . .' We had thought there might be some pipistrelle bats, which are tiny

(weighing only a few grams), not un-common in towns, and emit some sounds which can be heard without a bat detector. The noctule bat is much larger, with a wing-span that reaches about sixteen inches, and it eats large nocturnal insects, such as moths.

But even a large bat is not easy to see on a dull night, and for some time we would catch glimpses of them, while the detectors crackled more frequently. We moved to the edge of the Serpentine, where the police said they often saw bats lit up in their car headlights, and the noctules were everywhere, emerg-ing as jagged, jinking silhouettes quite close to us. The cameraman said there was no light, and, in vain the electrician shone his portable lamp – known as a 'sun-gun' – at the sky. It was very

Gardens are ideal for hedgehogs, and though some people will feed them catfood they live mainly on slugs and other insects.

frustrating. Here was a mammal right in the centre of London, living entirely on insects and roosting nobody knew quite where, and we could not get any film of it. We shot a few feet of film in the blackness, which when developed was a few feet of blackness.

We knew that if we were able to go somewhere that bats were studied and kept we could film them, and cut this in to the Hyde Park sequence with the bat detectors – a standard practice in wildlife films. But we really wanted to show the bats flying against the evening lights of Knightsbridge because it was such a thrilling sight. This was a recurring problem with our attempts to give a convincing portrait of creatures living wild in the urban landscape. If we were able to get close to a bird to film it, we could not see the context in which it was living – the shot was too narrow. If we framed up for a wide shot we could not see the bird. With the bats, we simply could not see anything.

The peak filming time was in June, when most of the birds are nesting, butterflies are about, and the light is good from early morning until late evening. That was the theory. In practice, the problems of following the unfolding of the seasons were far greater than we had feared. The spring was late, and it was the wettest June for twenty-five years. Birds have good and bad years for breeding, even in the town, and we had a bad year. Even when we found some activity, the dull light made it impossible to use long lenses for close-ups. On fine days, the wildlife cameramen were not always available, as they were stuck in a hide somewhere else in the country getting a sequence for someone else's film.

One of the greatest difficulties, however, was the behaviour of wildlife itself, for this proved to be very unpredictable. We never knew when any species of bird was going to nest, when the fox cubs would emerge from their earth, when the badgers would be out, and though scores of helpful observers would assure us that we could 'set our watch' by the habits of some creatures the wildlife cameraman went on a fruitless mission to film. When things do happen, they take place very quickly and timing is critical. A nest would be found with eggs in it – a hedge sparrow, for example, in Buckingham Palace Garden. So we would wait until the eggs hatched, because when the birds are 'sitting' on eggs there is little activity. When first hatched, the chicks are tiny, difficult to film, and there is a danger that the presence of the cameraman will make the parent birds abandon the nest. The best time was the few days when the large chicks are being fed. And you can be sure that on those days it would rain or the cameraman was not about, or everything was fine and ready to go and the nest was out of bounds for the week. These difficulties dogged us throughout the project, and we got a taste of them early on as we tried to tackle the winter months without quite knowing what to aim at.

In mid-winter, when we were still trying to form our ideas about the nature of urban wildlife and to identify the species we should film, there was a heavy snowfall. We knew that there were many birds which visited London from autumn until spring, and that the lakes, canals and reservoirs of the capital were a haven for wild ducks, wading birds, gulls and cormorants. In fact, we saw cormorants flying with a kind of long-necked prehistoric profile past our office window on the South Bank every day, following the Thames going east to west in the morning, and returning in the afternoon or evening to wheel around St Paul's Cathedral and head north.

When the snow came, we decided to capture the visually stunning sight of the reservoirs and urban wastes of the capital covered in white. We had heard

Cormorants roosting on an island at Walthamstow reservoirs in north London where large number now winter, feeding on fish in the Thames, and stealing anglers' trout from the reservoir.

that there was a good selection of birds at Walthamstow reservoirs, and that on the adjoining marshes there were kestrels and short-eared owls. This is an area in the Victorian suburbs of north London, in the valley of the River Lea which flows from countryside right through the industrial East End to the Thames. The short-eared owl does not breed in London, but quite a number of them move south in the winter from the east coast and further north in Europe. They are wonderful birds to look at: like small buzzards, with a moth-like flight as they quarter the ground in search of small mammals. And they fly by day, which means that they are a relatively easy to to film.

Before we began to make the film, a young birder gave us a tour of the Walthamstow marshes, and put up one of these owls, which had been roosting in the long, snow-covered grass. As it flew up, a carrion crow attacked it and drove it off. Then we spent a day at Walthamstow filming the wild duck, teal, tufted, pochard and the cormorants in the snow.

We moved on to the marshes in search of the owls. There were kestrels everywhere, and stonechats – small birds the size of a robin, and what birders classify as an 'LBJ', a little brown job as it is hard to distinguish them by sight in the field from similar species. The stonechats, heathland birds, seemed to follow us but did not want to be filmed. But no owl. A heavy snow shower caught us right in the middle of the marsh and a bitter wind froze us to the bone. We tramped on like stragglers from the failed expedition of Captain Scott until we came to the canal where the railway crossed it. As we stood, aimlessly it seemed in the blizzard, a field-mouse appeared and scampered frantically across the snow in search of food. It moved, so we tried to film it. At this point, two Lea Valley Regional Park rangers appeared, like

Yogi Bears from Yellowstone, and asked what we were doing. They said we ought to be filming the short-eared owls which they often watched from their landrover. We said we were, but we could not see it just at the moment, and thought a fieldmouse would fill in some time.

Then we shouted: 'Bewick's.' Without knowing quite what we meant, the cameraman swung round and with a long lens, shooting through the railway arches with the snow falling heavily, focussed on a family of swans which were landing on the canal like a vision from a fairy-tale. They swam around on the water for a few moments before a pair of mute swans – the kind commonly resident in London – approached them with raised wings and forced them off the canal. The Bewick's swans rose through the snow and with loping wings made off through the blizzard. It was an extraordinary sight, and very exciting, as the Bewick's swan, which breeds in Siberia, is a rare winter visitor to London, and the family had probably been driven further south than normal by the arctic conditions we were experiencing. When we saw the film it was breathtaking as the swans rose from the water and turned in the air against the backdrop of houses in Walthamstow.

We did not film the short-eared owls at Walthamstow, but we found them regularly at Rainham Marsh on the outskirts of London, near Dagenham, hunting close to a busy road which serves chemical factories and rubbish tips. This was an area we visited on many occasions, for it is a classic urban-industrial wildlife sanctuary, with its regular birders who religiously record the migrant species they find. Out of Rainham village, you cross the railway line. On the right are factories, and on the left a great expanse of tussocky grassland stretching to a bank which is the border with the raised sludge beds

One of the most spectacular winter visitors to London's rough grasslands, the short-eared owl which hunts voles.

into which the Port of London Authority pumps water from the Thames to keep it clear of silt. We saw the short-eared owls on our first visit, and many times after that, but wondered how close we could get to them in flight and whether they could be filmed against the backdrop of the factories.

One afternoon, we decided to give it a try. The owls were there, but the light was very bad and failing. However, an owl appeared at a bend in the road and began to hunt, flying low over the ground about twenty yards from us.

The cameraman picked it up and managed to follow it as it glided, hovered and dived only a few feet from the stream of cars and lorries going to and from the factories. It was, we thought, the perfect image of wildlife in the city.

Like many winter visitors to London, the short-eared owl eats only natural foods, and was further confirmation that wildlife in the city is not always scavenging. There were other magnificent birds like that on the marshes: hen-harriers, for example. We saw a male bird, which has an eerie silver-

A short-eared owl quarters Rainham Marsh in industrial east London.

blue colouring, on several occasions, which might have been preying on any of the birds wintering on the sludge beds including the snipe. We also saw short-eared owls and hen-harriers on the artificial heathlands that have become established on the overgrown rubbish-tips near Rainham.

In winter, as in spring and summer, the city provides wildlife with food and shelter. As in the countryside the seasons bring a great change to the city. In winter, suburban hedgehogs hibernate, red foxes move their territory and become bolder, wild plants wither and die. The summer visitors have all gone: the house martins, swifts and swallows have returned to Africa. So too have such birds as fly-catchers and white-throats. But many more birds arrive. Northern thrushes, the fieldfares and redwings appear in the parks and gardens of the city. From a distance they look like our thrushes, but close-to the fieldfare has a beautiful smokey-grey colouring, and the redwing rich reddy brown speckles and a vivid eye stripe. Tens of thousands of European starlings join the resident population. Seagulls and wild duck feed alongside the ornamental species in Regent's Park and Hyde Park.

Even in London Zoo, the wildlife changes with the seasons, as the migrant birds move in. The wild creatures of the city are locked into a natural world: the urban landscape is part of the whole landscape of Britain, and its green islands are not as different from patches of countryside as is often imagined. The extraordinary variety of wildlife that can be found in the city is a function of the range of habitats that can be found there: grassland, woodland, heathland, canals, lakes, rivers. For example, the short-eared owl and the stonechat need open ground and long grass, and you can expect to find them wherever there is a sufficient stretch of this kind of vegetation, whether it is a Scottish moor, or an overgrown rubbish-tip. The short-eared owls might breed in London were it not for the disturbance they are likely to suffer in the spring. And there might be many more small mammals for short-eared owls to eat, if much of the grassland of the capital were allowed to grow long to provide voles and wood-mice with the cover they need.

You can apply to green islands in the city exactly the same basic ecological principles usually reserved for apparently 'wilder' places. This might seem to be a very obvious point, but it took us some while to be convinced of it, and to overcome a conventional assumption that any wildlife that lives in the city is somehow fundamentally *different* from wildlife in the country-side. It is not. However, it is easy to exaggerate the value and potential of the city for wildlife. As more urban foxes have been unearthed in recent years, and the wealth of wild creatures that can be found in town has been publicised, a false view that the city is now *better* for wildlife than the country-side has gained some currency. An argument which we have read a number of times runs roughly along the following lines. Farmers have destroyed more and more of the hedgerows and woodlands of the country, driving out the wild creatures and forcing them to look for new pastures. Responding to the onslaught in the country, many animals have 'moved into town'. The image is of an exodus of a rural population into the city, rather like the human migrations in the eighteenth and nineteenth centuries. Soon, all the wildlife will be living in towns, and rural nests will be deserted.

This is not what has happened; except in a few special cases. Richmond Park, or any tract of suburbia, is certainly less hostile to much wildlife than a vast ploughed field in East Anglia. But there is a smaller range of wildlife

The red fox has become a symbol of urban wildlife, and is very common. It does scavenge food from man, but also eats wild birds, mice, worms and fruit.

in the city than there is in the country-side. When a new species appears to move in to town it is often not because it is running away from rural areas, but because its numbers have greatly increased in the countryside and the population pressure has pushed it into the city. But not all wildlife can find what it needs in the city: some species do very well while others seem unable to exploit its natural resources. The reasons why some wildlife makes it into town and some does not is the subject of our next chapter.

ISLANDS IN THE CITY

O N A DAY in February we were
looking out of our office window on the twenty-second
floor when a crow flew by and glided
across the Thames. It was carrying a
twig in its beak, and we watched it turn
over the traffic on the Embankment
and land in a tall plane tree. The leaves
were not yet out on the tree, and with
binoculars we could see the shape of a
crow's nest, something we had been
looking for in central London in a place
where we could film it. This particular
nest seemed to be ideal, for it was quite
close to a building with a balcony. And
the crows raised young there, with our
cameraman watching, on this tiny island of greenery by the Thames with
traffic roaring below.

We were interested in the carrion
crow because as a species it is very
successful in London; nearly every central square has a pair nesting high up in
a plane tree. The thin strip of greenery
called the Embankment Gardens, hemmed in by two lanes of traffic on one
side, and a solid mass of buildings on
the other is enough, with its plane trees,
to support several pairs of crows. The
contents of rubbish barges moored in
the middle of the Thames provide a
good source of food for the growing
young. Later in the spring, we had a
look around in the shrubs below our
particular crows' nest, and in no time
had found a woodpigeon feeding its
young, a blackbird nesting in full view
of passers-by – though few seemed to
notice it – and a hedge sparrow sitting
on eggs deep in a bush. It was quite

remarkable what this one small patch
of greenery in such a disturbed area
could support in the way of wildlife.

But how could we explain why some
species had managed to colonise this
little island, while others were absent?
Applied to London as a whole this
proved to be the biggest and most
puzzling question about city wildlife,
and it led us off in a number of different
directions, and took us eventually into
the Buckingham Palace Garden.

An aerial view of any city shows
islands of greenery, set in a sea of
concrete and bustling human activity.

The carrion crow at its nest, feeding young, high above the traffic on the Embankment.

So, if any particular species were to survive in the city it has to make it to one of these islands, and if it is to become resident there, the island would have to be big enough to support it. True islands in the ocean have interested zoologists for a long time, because their isolation has given rise to some unusual communities of species. Cut off from the mainstream of evolution on the continents, islands have harboured some strange and archaic birds, such as the flightless dodo and the kiwi, or marsupials (such as the kangaroo) which carry their young in pouches, long after these had become extinct on the mainland masses. This has happened over millions of years. Nobody would expect city islands to support unique species comparable to those on oceanic islands because towns are simply not old or isolated enough. But there are interesting comparisons between oceanic and urban islands which are more relevant.

There is the case of the volcanic island Krakatoa in the East Indies which erupted in 1883. The volcanic ash was in some places 100 feet thick, and everything was destroyed; absolutely nothing survived there. But within a few years, things began to turn up — the first creature to arrive was a spider. After fifty years, as well as the spiders there were 720 species of insect recorded, thirty breeding birds, and a few species of reptile and mammal living in the regenerating jungle forest. All these colonisers had had to make a journey across the sea from the nearest land twenty-five miles away on the islands of Java and Sumatra. This was an impressive effort, though the range of creatures which had colonised Krakatoa half a century after the eruption was considerably less than could be found on less disturbed and larger nearby islands.

With a little bit of imagination it is possible to view the building of a great city like London in much the same way. From 1815 it expanded at a tremendous pace, covering the countryside in bricks and mortar. It continued to grow until 1939 when the outer limits of semi-detached suburbia were reached at the outbreak of the Second World War. Not very much could have survived this onslaught as trees were felled and fields were dug up and covered in concrete. Some expanses of original green were left as the lava flow of building development spread round them, leaving a few durable species marooned and surrounded by concrete, but they became more and more isolated from the countryside. However, as the lava flow of building ceased and the landscape began to settle down, the islands of greenery in the city became more peaceful and a recolonisation from the countryside began.

If rural areas around a large city are compared with any of the green islands within the built-up parts of town, it is generally true that the countryside has a greater *range* of wildlife in it than the town. The reason for this is that only a limited number of species has been able to 'get in' to town, and to find on one of its green islands the kind of food and shelter that it needs to survive there. Now this raises a host of interesting and very difficult questions about why some creatures have been successful at extending their range from the countryside into the town while others have not. There seem to be two different, possible explanations.

It could be that the successful colonising species, such as blackbirds, evolved new characteristics which enabled them to tolerate life in suburban gardens and parks. The private life of all wild creatures is extremely complicated, and there are many small changes which could occur in a few individuals in their feeding habits, their timidity, or choice of nesting-sites, which might turn an essentially rural

Buckingham Palace Garden is like an island of greenery in the city, with a remarkable range of wildlife. Many wild plants take root here – the tall Japanese knotweed rises above bluebells and daffodils.

bird into a successful town bird. We have discussed this possibility later in the chapter.

However, there is an alternative explanation which we found generally more plausible. What scanty evidence there is seems to support the idea that the behaviour patterns, or 'life-style', of wild birds and animals has not altered much during the period in which towns have been built – 150 years or so. Birds that nested high in trees continue to do so; those that nest on the ground continue to do so; bad-

The London plane tree, a cross between two alien species, provides some wildlife with a haven on the Embankment.

gers live in communal 'setts' – a complex of burrows – and red foxes are more mobile, moving their solitary 'earths' more frequently. So we imagined, for the sake of argument, that no amazing adaptations had occurred. Those wild creatures that colonised towns successfully did so because their numbers were growing in the countryside, and when some moved into urban areas they found the habitat they needed to survive.

If this is the case, then what limits the range of wildlife in towns is not whether adaptation has taken place in individual species, but the extent and variety of vegetation or habitats that can be found in towns and how closely these approximate to the conditions any plants or animals need to survive. It follows from this that the green islands of the city will vary in the amount and variety of wildlife they support.

A very large 'green island', with many old trees, plenty of scrub and thicket, as well as mown and long grass, will support more species than a much smaller island with less variety in its vegetation. The distance of any island from the surrounding countryside is also critical for some species which travel overland, because they might have a long way to go to reach it. So, using as a model the volcanic island of Krakatoa, we began to speculate on how various plants and animals might make the journey from the 'mainland' (the countryside) to an urban island in the 'ocean' of a city's built-up area.

What we first needed was an island in London that had been extensively studied by naturalists so that we had as complete a record as possible of all the birds, mammals, reptiles, wild plants, insects and other creatures which could be found there. This proved to be difficult, for even if you were to step out into your back garden to survey its flora and fauna it would take a considerable time, and nobody had undertaken a comprehensive survey of any of the large parks or open spaces in the city. There were regular 'bird reports' for the Royal Parks – those now administered by the Government – but nothing on the mammals or insects of, say, Hyde Park.

We could find only one city island of any size that had been thoroughly surveyed, and this turned out to be, remarkably, Buckingham Palace Garden. More than twenty years ago, a team of naturalists had got permission to explore the great lawns, ornamental shrubberies, the lake and the wilder, untended areas of Her Majesty the Queen's private back garden. Their discoveries about the kinds of wildlife to be found there were fascinating, and provided us with the kind of 'model' we needed for an urban island.

Of course, Buckingham Palace Garden is unlike any other large open space in central London. Though crowded when royal garden parties are held on the enormous lawns, it is eerily quiet at other times; the roar of traffic on the busy roads around muted and muffled by the high security wall, the edifice of the Palace itself, and the tall trees which grow there. On the few visits we were able to make, the entire thirty-nine acres were more or less deserted, with only the gardeners or policemen – some of whom can be seen pedalling bicycles rather comically in the distance – patrolling the gravel paths.

When we were finally given permission to see the garden, we were able to take as a guide the naturalist David McClintock who had led the team which carried out the wildlife survey more than twenty years ago. Also with us was Stanley Cramp, one of the great experts on birds in inner London. He, with McClintock, has kept up his interest in the Palace grounds, visiting them a few times each year in the early morning, to look for migrant birds and any new arrivals amongst the breeding

A mallard duck on her nest amongst building materials in Buckingham Palace Garden. Palace police will help shepherd her brood to St James's Park.

DO NOT DISTURB
BIRD NESTS

species there. Since the first survey, one thing had changed radically – the security system at the Palace. We all had to wait to have our photographs taken for an identity card, and both our venerable guides who had been popping in to see what was new for all those years were rather unceremoniously quizzed, made to sit in the mug-shot chair and handed clip-on passes before we were let loose in the Garden.

Here we met Fred Kemp, a gardener with a keen interest in wildlife and an invaluable source of information about plants and nests, and we were able to wander about the extensive grounds quite freely. We had with us the results of the first survey, published in 1964 in the *South London Entomological and Natu-*ral *History Society's Proceedings*. At the time the survey was carried out the Palace did not want the results published and would allow them to go into print only in an obscure publication. Unaccountably, the *London Naturalist* turned them down.

It is just as well we had this survey with us, because on that first visit in April we saw very few birds and no other animals at all, and it might have been easy to form the impression that this was – apart from the plants – a kind of desert island in the city. Though it was a beautiful day in April, spring was late and the nesting of many birds delayed. What we chiefly had to look at were the early flowering wild plants, and the ducks and geese on the lake.

Some nesting birds get special protection in the Palace Garden.

Though it is a wonderful wildlife reserve, the Palace Garden can support fewer creatures than most countryside because of its size, vegetation and the distance from rural areas.

It may seem odd that there are any *wild* plants in a place like Buckingham Palace Garden, for these are, for the most part, what gardeners call weeds. Though most of the grounds are planted with some very attractive shrubs and flowers and are well tended, there are many patches where self-seeded plants can get a hold. The lake in the garden is quite large, with 'natural' banks, and on these David McClintock was able to point out a number of wild plants. One of the first we saw was coltsfoot, a yellow dandelion-like flower common on wasteground, and next to it Japanese knotweed, an introduced species from Asia which grows all over London and may have been planted here years ago as an ornamental plant, subsequently 'gone wild'.

David McClintock, carrying a plastic bag in which to pop interesting specimens, searched the ground, while Stanley Cramp scanned the trees with his binoculars. Fred Kemp showed us a nest built in the creeper by the head gardener's house, with four eggs in it. This belonged to a dunnock, or hedge sparrow – a small bird often mistaken for a female house sparrow, but with a different dusky colouring, very different habitats and a rather attractive tinkling song. There was a mallard duck nesting at the back of the garden sheds amongst some old concrete blocks, a robin's nest hidden deep in a small bush, but not much else. A couple of passage migrant birds went through – a chiffchaff, the little warbler that is often heard but less often seen, hunting insects high up in the trees, and a pied fly-catcher, a rare summer visitor from Africa, which was stopping off to feed on its way to a more favourable and distant breeding territory.

But the overwhelming impression was one of quiet, and this produced in us a kind of terror. If it was like this when we came to film what would we be able to show? Very little. For the Gar-

den is very large, and it would take days and weeks – the sort of concentrated study David McClintock's five-year survey provided – to identify even a small part of the wildlife there. Even in the centre of a large town, in ornamental gardens like these, wildlife is inconspicuous. David McClintock's team in the early 1960s was composed of specialists on plants, birds and butterflies and moths, mammals and spiders, while his own expert knowledge took care of the plants. Their findings were quite extraordinary. More than 260 species of wild plant were found in the original survey, and David McClintock has added to that list since – he even made a discovery while we were filming there on a dismally wet day in June. This 'list', though it included some oddities and rarities, is not as impressive as it sounds, for central London, in which a certain group of fast-travelling, nomadic plants do very well on wasteground. As nearly all of these plants are what we would call weeds, it was touching to observe McClintock the botanist asking Mr Kemp, the interested gardener, to preserve a particular species from the hoe until it could be positively identified!

Some of the weeds, common along the roadsides everywhere, are very pretty. The ox-eye daisies, which grow in profusion on a bank of the lake, make a fine show, as does one of the commonest of urban 'ruderal' plants (a fancy terms for weeds), the yellow Oxford ragwort, about which there is much more in Chapter Three. There was also hemlock water dropwort, a poisonous plant, and the beautiful white dead nettle in flower. This last looks like a nettle but does not sting, and has pretty white flowers on the stem which when upturned reveal an attractive pattern, similar in colouring to a black-eyed bean.

For the most part, it is not difficult to guess how these plants got into the

Garden, though it is impossible to know in each case how they arrived, for there are several possibilities. Quite a few, like the ragwort, produce tiny seeds with wispy parachutes which are carried everywhere by the wind. In other words, they fly into the Garden, and will take root and seed on most untended ground. Many other plants probably arrived on the shoes or clothes of visitors to garden parties. A great many potting plants are brought in to add colour to the Garden and the soil in which they arrive will often contain weed seeds. Birds will often transport seeds from one place to another, either by eating them and depositing them in droppings, or perhaps attached to mud on their feet. David McClintock has also made a special study of the plants that grow from birdseed put out on one of the balconies of Buckingham Palace; he checks each year for exotic varieties which have taken root.

While we were filming, his eagle eye spotted a new arrival amongst the ox-eye daisies and Oxford ragwort. This was chervil, a tall parsley-like plant with feathery leaves, which David McClintock picked and ate – pronouncing it a delicious herb – having made sure of its identity in his field

The wild flowers of the Palace Garden grow in untended areas – this is common ragwort by the lake.

Canada geese, introduced to England from North America, try to breed in the Palace Garden, but are not encouraged.

guide. We were also shown one of the great puzzles of the garden: a relative of the ferns called adder's tongue, which had popped up a few years ago in a quiet corner by the lake. It is a puzzle, because it is used as an indicator of old meadowland and here it was in a garden in the centre of London, making an unexpected appearance.

The plants are the easiest form of wildlife to find and identify, and, though more difficult, the birds are second in order of conspicuousness. The great difficulty with them is finding a nest to actually *prove* they are breeding there.

Over three years in the early 1960s, the Palace survey identified over twenty species of breeding bird – an impressive number for such a small area so far from the countryside. These included all the common garden birds: robins, dunnocks, blackbirds, thrushes, woodpigeons, blue tits and great tits. The lake provided an aquatic breeding ground for a number of species of duck, as well as the Canada goose, which has not been welcomed because its cropping of the grass tends to turn it into mud and it leaves enormous droppings which are liable to soil the polished shoes of visitors and, unaccountably, are rumoured to be the favoured food of the royal corgis. So Canada geese – seen in all the parks, black-and-white striped, honking manically all the time and rather aggressive – *try* to nest in the Garden, and could do so easily if their eggs were not removed to foil their colonisation plans.

The carrion crows, which can often be seen around the Palace, also try to nest there, and perhaps do so successfully, but they are discouraged with gunfire because they are thought to have too healthy a taste for the ducklings, whether of the wild mallard or the ornamental species kept with clipped wings on the lake. On one of our visits, a crow had caused a problem by trigger-ing an alarm system in its flight round the buildings.

Among the birds there is nothing very rare in the Palace Garden, but the species list does include some timid birds which are summer migrants to Europe. One of these is the spotted flycatcher, which annually migrates from Africa to breed in Britain. One or two pairs nest each year in the Garden, and though we did not find the nest we were able to film these small, twitchy little insect-eaters hawking flies and other grubs among the willow trees by the lake. It is difficult to describe such birds. They are about the size of a robin, with a tawny kind of colouring and a slender beak. Their most distinguishing characteristic is the habit of sitting on a prominent perch and making quick sorties into the air to catch an insect, then returning to the same spot to eat it.

Many more birds visit the Garden than actually nest there. Herons will often fly in to hunt fish in the lake (what fish we do not know, because they were not surveyed) or to snap up a duckling or two, which they swallow whole. From late summer until spring, black-headed gulls – the most common of the five gull species found in London – will feed on the lawns. While we were filming outside the Palace we saw a kestrel hover overhead. During the spring and autumn migrations, many more birds than have ever been spotted will doubtless pass through the Garden, as they do through the nearby parks.

We were chiefly interested in the nesting birds as these are the true indicators of the range of species a city island will support, and on that count birds did by far the best of all the larger groups of animals. The variety of species here was not much different from that in the nearby acres of the much larger Hyde Park, but the *density* – the nesting pairs per acre – was very high, triple that of the Royal Parks, mainly because the Palace Garden is so quiet.

However, it was quite a different story with the mammals. The original survey had found practically none at all. On one occasion, David McClintock and his expert mammologist were certain they saw a vole in the gardens – 'Goodness, there's a vole!' they exclaimed, according to McClintock's account – but they never saw it again. They recorded no rabbits, or foxes, or badgers; not even grey squirrels which are found in large numbers in the nearby parks. Only two species, the house mouse and brown rat, were definitely recorded. There were almost certainly pipistrelle bats which also occur in Hyde Park.

By the early 1980s, the grey squirrels had arrived, though they are another unwelcome species as they eat the crocus bulbs – on our first visit a squirrel trap was set at the base of a tree in which there was a drey, a squirrel's nest of leaf and twigs. A single crocus bloomed in this cage which had clearly failed to trap a squirrel.

In this comparison of the relative success of birds and mammals in the Garden was the beginning of some confirmation of our working theory about the way in which wildlife colonises towns, and why some species get in and others do not. Wild plants and birds, broadly speaking, did much better than mammals. A very obvious explanation was that birds found it easier to get here simply because they could fly; and plants too had their own form of aerial distribution, as well as plenty of help with transport from man.

Buckingham Palace Garden was first enclosed by a high wall about 150 years ago. We have no idea what wildlife there was inside the wall at that time, or what was just outside the wall in the open country to the west where the new, stucco-clad houses of Belgravia were being built. But it is fair to assume that what was there then has little relevance to what is there now. Practically nothing, except perhaps for some insects and the odd plant, could have survived all those years as a tiny, isolated population cut off from the outside world.

Any species well established in the Garden would require constant topping up and recolonisation from the much larger and more stable population outside the walls, which means new individuals have to be able to get in to the Garden. The problem of getting there today from the countryside is now much greater, because London has grown so enormously around the Palace, ten miles at least in all directions.

The Garden's isolation could explain some absentees. How could a badger get there, for example, through all that traffic? A fox might make it, and they have got very close, but the high wall remains an obstacle. The grey squirrels managed to get in because of their ability to use the trees as an aerial highway. At several points along Constitution Hill, which runs from Hyde Park Corner down the side of the Garden, the branches of the trees outside the wall form a bridge where they touch the branches of trees inside. This is where the grey squirrels cross.

However, isolation presents no problems to the birds. What limits their numbers is the size of the Garden – palatial to the average Londoner, but small as wildlife reserves go – and the range of *habitats* offered in the thirty-nine acres. As in the rest of London, what this Garden most closely resembles in crude structure of scattered trees, lawns and shrubs, is woodland edge, suitable for birds like thrushes, robins and blackbirds. There is plenty of insect food on the vegetation, a wide range of nest sites for birds which build in trees and shrubs, and a lake for the ducks. However, quite a few 'habitats'

are missing – there is no heathland, or meadow, or dense woodland. There is nowhere, for example, for skylarks to nest in long grass on the ground, and probably not the food for them either.

In broad terms, the other findings of the original Palace survey seemed to confirm these rather obvious points. The moths and butterflies which have found their way into the garden have been monitored continuously for twenty years, and are still collected by John Bradley of the Natural History Museum. A moth trap – a bright light which attracts the night insects and

ensnares them for examination the next day – has been operated at the back of the Garden since the original survey, and is now the second largest, continuously operated trap of its kind in the country. These flying insects have no trouble getting to the garden and almost six hundred species of butterfly and moth have been caught here.

As with the birds, some of these moths and butterflies are migrants; red admirals, for instance, can overwinter rarely, but most are migrants from Southern Europe and North Africa. At least nine kinds of moth lay their eggs

A courting display by Canada geese in the Palace Garden, which will be fruitless. The eggs of these birds are destroyed because they foul the lawns with their droppings.

on grasses, which are the food-plants of their larvae (caterpillars), and the other vegetation in the garden would certainly support different species. The *Lepidoptera* – the scientific term for these insects – do quite well.

Spiders were also abundant when the original survey was carried out. There were fifty-seven different species found here, including a couple of rarities. How any of them actually got in to the Garden it is not possible to say, but spiders are good at climbing over walls, and in some species the young migrate to new territories by 'ballooning'. They spin threads of silk which, when long enough, catch the breeze and carry the tiny spiders into the air. Sometimes, hundreds of these balloonists are seen together on dewy grass, and it is their silk threads which are the gossamer of the fairies.

In general, insects and spiders are abundant in cities and this is reflected in the Palace Garden. What limits the insects is the amount and variety of vegetation, and the tidiness of most gardens in which rotting timber and leaf litter are taken away. However, there are other groups of animals, the amphibians and reptiles – frogs, toads, lizards and snakes – which did not appear in the Palace Garden though Fred Kemp the gardener remembered seeing frogs there. The lake may not be the kind of pond frogs and toads need to breed and there would be great mortality for the young, of frogs at least, as ducks like to eat spawn, tadpoles and grown adults and the population of these birds is artificially high. Without frogs to eat, and a plentiful supply of small fish, a grass snake is unlikely to survive, even if it did get in and was tolerated. Grass snakes also require very specific breeding sites, like compost heaps, which act as incubators for their delicate eggs.

If any conclusion can be drawn from the absence of amphibians and reptiles, it is perhaps that it is not only difficult for them to get into the Palace grounds but, if they did, they would have a struggle to survive there because of the large number of predators, as well as a lack of suitable breeding sites. So another important factor affecting the range of wildlife on city islands might therefore be the imbalance of species. Because bird numbers are not controlled in the Palace Garden, the survival chances of insects, frogs and toads might be affected.

Since the original survey twenty years ago, the only new arrivals recorded in the Garden have been among the plants, insects and birds. Since the 1970s, magpies have invaded many towns including central London, and they are now established in the garden, waddling over the lawns in their black and white plumage. Long-tailed tits have almost certainly nested there, as they have done in Hyde Park, though we could not find a nest. All in all, the wildlife of the garden remains unba-

Tawny owls have been seen and heard in Buckingham Palace Garden. But there's no record of them nesting there.

lanced because of the difficulties of colonisation for some species, a typical characteristic of oceanic and urban islands.

The wildlife of Buckingham Palace Garden is not very impressive in its range when compared with open countryside, but it is quite extraordinary when measured against its central position, and what can be found immediately outside the Palace gates. There, where the guard is changed ritually, every morning, to the delight of the tourists who flock to the Victoria Memorial and the iron railings outside the Palace to see the soldiers in their quaint red uniforms and beaver hats marching through the traffic (Zelda Fitzgerald, dotty wife of the famous American author described the scene as: 'The Town Hall with Redskins walking round it') there is hardly any wildlife at all.

Although it is possible to talk generally about 'urban wildlife' as if there were a distinct group of species found everywhere in towns, wild creatures are, in fact, distributed very unevenly because of their reliance on islands of greenery. In the rockiest, noisiest areas outside the Palace, there are no mammals (other than perhaps sewer rats underground), only three or four species of breeding birds, a few insects and a weed or two growing between the cracks in the paving-stones. To find more than that, you have to go to the parks, gardens, wastegrounds, golf courses or some patch of vegetation, which is vital for most species found in the city.

One of the most pleasing experiences on our safari was climbing into the landrover of David Smith, ex-taxi driver and now gamekeeper in Richmond Park, and leaving the road to drive across the rough turf past herds of red and fallow deer towards one of the great stands of oak trees. The 2,500 acres of woodland and rough grassland of Rich-

Caught in the moth trap operated in the Palace Garden the poplar hawk moth, little seen because it flies by night.

Aglais urticae L.
Small Tortoiseshell

Inachis io L.
Peacock

Vanessa atalanta L.
Red Admiral

Vanessa cardui L.
Painted Lady

Pieris rapae L.
Small Garden White

Pieris brassicae L.
Large Garden White

Gonepteryx rhamni L.
Brimstone

Mimas tiliae L.
Lime Hawk

Laothoe populi L.
Poplar Hawk

Sphinx ligustri L.
Privet Hawk

Pararge aegeria
Speckled Wood

Deilephila elpenor L.
Elephant Hawk-moth

Phalera bucephala L.
Buff-tip

Tethea ocularis L.

Drepana lac
Scalloped H

Cilix gla
Chinese

Orgyia ar
Common

Euproctis c
Brown-tail

Leucom
White

Nola cuculla
Short-cloake

Eilema l
Common

Eilema
Scarce

Spilos
(lubric
Buff E

Spiloson
(mentha
White E

Cycni
Musli

A collection held by John Bradley at the Natural History Museum of some of the hundreds of moths and butterflies trapped in the Palace Garden.

mond Park, cut off from the countryside by suburbia, form the largest of London's green islands, though this is not a natural landscape. The whole place is managed as a deer park, and it is reminiscent of Scotland in places. We had asked about the possibility of badgers living in the park, and were surprised to learn that there was not just one badger sett, but possibly as many as twenty. There was one among the trees of a fenced enclosure, another just off one of the main roads, another by the golf course. David Smith is a keen wildlife photographer and showed us many pictures of the badgers caught in his flashlight as they emerged from their burrows in the evening. We examined the setts, saw evidence of fresh digging, the tidy mound of badger droppings – but we never saw the beast itself.

There are also plenty of foxes in Richmond Park, which had been photographed in broad daylight by David Smith. So, here we had the perfect comparison, on a large city island, of two animals, one of which could get to Richmond Park and no further, and the other which penetrated London virtually to the gates of Buckingham Palace. Why had the fox moved so far into the town and left the badger behind?

A simple comparison of the two animals provided a straight forward kind of answer. Badgers live in colonies comprising several adults. To dig their setts, an elaborate series of tunnels, they need sandy soil. This limits their distribution in the countryside as much as in the town. They are very powerful, stocky animals, which tend to move at night along fixed routes and wear a discernible path to and from the sett. Their diet is made up largely of earthworms but they will also eat a range of other items from slugs to hedgehogs.

Fallow deer in Richmond Park, the largest and in many ways the wildest of green islands within London's built-up areas. A much wider range of wildlife can survive here than in the Palace Garden.

They are not very agile and when they come to an obstacle they usually burrow under it: they are not built for climbing. So badgers are quite specific in their requirements and once established they will stay in the same place for many years, as the colony and number of badgers expands.

Red foxes, on the other hand, are by nature much more mobile and less specific in their requirements. They are more solitary than the badger and can live almost unnoticed even in a city garden. They are very agile, can jump quite high walls and fences, and will eat almost anything they can find. The clichéd picture of urban wildlife shows a fox sniffing round an overturned dustbin. The text then usually refers to the fox having adapted to town life, as if by genetic mutation a new dustbin-sniffing strain of fox had arisen (*Vulpes dustbinicus*). Studies of rural foxes show just the same kind of scavenging behaviour, and there is a great deal of food available to foxes in town which does not come from dustbins. They eat worms, beetles, fruit such as blackberries, ducks, mice and rabbits – all of which are everywhere, including Hyde Park.

It is really no great puzzle that the fox has been able to penetrate towns and can thrive in suburbia: it has long been associated with man, even stealing his chickens in the country. It is a species which is, in a sense, pre-adapted to urban life. But what is difficult to piece together is the history of the arrival of foxes in towns, and exactly how the colonisation began.

If you take the story back thousands

A red fox with cubs born in suburban earth, dug out under an old air-raid shelter in south London suburbia.

of years, before any large towns were built and Britain as a country was still thickly wooded, the red fox was probably a creature of woodland edge and not all that common. Even then, foxes probably survived on a very wide range of foods. As the forests were cleared, and many more specialised animals began to disappear, the red fox – along with many other animals which were adapted to woodland edge – probably did very well and its numbers increased. But during the nineteenth century, persecution by farmers and gamekeepers kept its numbers down, and by the turn of this century it was not all that common.

Fox hunters took to breeding and importing foxes from Europe to provide themselves with sport, and it is likely that the rural population of the fox increased as a result, and did well during the First World War when the activities of gamekeepers in the countryside diminished as countrymen went off to fight in the trenches. After the Great War, when the semi-detached suburbs of London and other large towns were built – with many more gardens and a much lower density of housing – the fox was doing well in the countryside, and some might actually have been enclosed by the rapid building of suburbia. Whereas the suburban back garden was not much use to the badger – when setts appear in the middle of people's lawns they generally get rid of them – the fox could roam freely through this new territory.

When any species is doing well its

The common lizard is found on a few of London's islands: we found this one near Wormwood Scrubs.

numbers increase at an accelerating rate, and this was almost certainly the case with the fox when there was a traumatic event in the countryside: myxomatosis. This disease decimated the rabbit population of the English countryside in a few years, and thousands of bobbing tails in the fields disappeared. It has sometimes been suggested that the fox then abandoned the countryside, and moved in to town in search of food. But it is more likely that the maimed and blinded millions of rabbits hit by myxomatosis temporarily increased the foxes' food supply, increased its numbers, and the move in to town was a search for new territory by a growing population.

Foxes mate in the winter, when the cries of the vixen, like the shriek of a murder victim startle and often annoy people as far into London as the Victorian suburbs of Putney or Wimbledon. The cubs are born in the earth in early spring, but do not take their first look at the outside world until April, roundabout the time the first bluebells are in flower. They emerge in the evenings to play near the earth and to be suckled by the vixen. There are many generations of foxes now born into suburbia, and they will set off later in the year to establish new territory; probably in a nearby garden as related foxes, especially females, do not disperse very far.

We were lucky enough to be able to watch and film fox cubs suckling and playing in a back garden in Sidcup. Everyone, of course, knew there were foxes about, and we would often be told one could be seen on this railway embankment or that, but they were never predictable. Quite often, when people have encouraged foxes to visit or live in their back gardens they do not want anyone filming them because neighbours object to the animals. There was a good deal of disagreement about whether or not foxes were welcome in the suburbs where we filmed.

The main obstacles to foxes moving in to towns appear to be people and stray dogs. In Europe, where foxes are carriers of rabies, they are gassed and kept out of towns. In Britain nobody has controlled them, and they have no natural competitors. Research in Bristol has suggested that foxes are much more common in middle-class areas than on council estates because they will not go where there are many stray dogs. It is also possible that since the turn of the century the number of stray dogs in towns has decreased, and this has helped the foxes.

While we were researching this project, a fox was caught in an office block near Tower Bridge during the winter. It is likely that foxes move further in to the centre when the weather is hard, and they roam more during the winter. We also heard of foxes being shot in Holland Park and Regent's Park the year before, because they had killed some of the ornamental birds. A report that foxes were regularly seen at the Hurlingham Club was followed up, and we were told 'an old fox' had been shot there two years before. But the earth nearest to the centre of town that we actually found was in Hyde Park.

As far as we could see, this earth was no longer in use – no fresh paw marks, no distinct foxy smell, and no kills. However we wanted to show a fox in the centre of town, and resorted to the standard wildlife filming ruse of importing a captive animal. It was *not* tame, like a dog, and was virtually impossible to handle in this setting as it turned out, but on the day we tried to re-create the scene of the foxes in Hyde Park, the earth was once again in use – above it were two, freshly chewed wings of a small bird.

The fox is often used as a talisman of urban wildlife, and rightly so because its story, as far as we understand it, is that of many animals which have colonised towns. On the other hand, the badger is unlikely to have much success and may well be on the retreat, for the sett which used to be at Kenwood on Hampstead Heath, has now gone. Badgers can only be found in large numbers on the very fringes of the built-up area. It is not that they have failed to adapt to the town; rather the town does not provide what they need. An exception to this was a badger sett shown to us way out of town at Pitsea in Essex, one of the huge land-filled dumps that had taken London's rubbish in the 1960s and was now covered with earth. There badgers had dug out an earth under an electricity pylon, burrowing in to evocative layers of broken records, bottles and nylon stockings!

Much of the wildlife that can be found in Richmond Park is, like the badger, confined to the largest city islands or the rural fringe of the capital. This appears to be because there is some specific requirement lacking in towns. One rather puzzling example, however, is the jackdaw, a bird very much associated with church spires in small country towns. The jackdaw is a

Badgers do well in places like Richmond Park and on the outskirts of London, but, unlike foxes, have not been able to move into the centre.

small crow, with a slightly comical waddle as it walks, a slate grey head, and a characteristic cry of 'Jack-Jack'. When we first saw them in Richmond Park, where there is a colony breeding in the old oak trees, they were hopping onto the backs of ruminating red deer and pulling out their moulting fur. The hair stuck out either side of the jackdaws' beaks, giving them the appearance of mad moustachioed colonels. They flew off with the hair to their nests in tree-holes.

A few years ago, there was a colony of jackdaws in Kensington Gardens, but they are gone now and the Richmond Park birds seem to be the established group closest to central London. What confines this species here is not clear – it might be food, for they eat a great many grubs, or it might be nesting material, or more likely nest-sites. Thousands of elm trees were killed by disease in the central parks in the 1970s. These had provided the jackdaws with nest-holes and when these trees were removed it could be that competition for alternative sites from other species, such as the London pigeon, kept them out. The mystery remains.

Close to the crows' nest we filmed on the Embankment was the site of the last rookery in central London which disappeared in 1916. The felling of tall trees in Kensington Gardens and elsewhere in the nineteenth century was much criticised by naturalists as it appeared to be driving out the rooks, which build their nests very high up in large colonies. But the real reason for

A kestrel chick flexes its wings in a cramped nest in the heating and vent shaft of a tower block in Wembley.

their disappearance is more likely to be their relatively specialised food supply, especially when they feed their young in the very early spring. They favour agricultural land where they feed in flocks on grubs and insects, and will fly quite long distances to find them. As London grew around their central nest-sites, the distance between the rookery and the first farmland would have become greater until the daily journey became too much and they left.

Provided an animal can find a place to breed and the food it needs, the treetops and the rooftops of a city are a relatively hospitable place. This is the territory of one of London's most colourful and exciting colonisers – the kestrel, a small falcon. It is often confused with a similar sized bird of prey, the sparrow hawk, which from its name you would expect to do well in sparrow-ridden London. But there are very few sparrow hawks in London, and it is worth asking why this is. The crucial difference between the sparrow hawk – which will nest on the larger city islands such as Richmond Park and Kew Gardens – and the kestrel is their method of hunting and their favoured nest-sites.

Whereas the sparrow hawk will fly low over hedgerows or walls, swoop up to surprise a group of small birds and grab one in the air or on the ground, the kestrel has the extraordinary ability to hover in the air, remaining absolutely stationary even in a high wind. This enables the kestrel to hunt in the mountainous landscape of the city whereas even in the countryside the sparrow hawk is well known for crashing into unseen windows as it chases its prey. In addition, kestrels will nest high up in or on buildings – just as they can nest on cliffs in rural areas – whereas the sparrow hawk favours trees. The kestrel's nest we filmed was at the top of a tower block in Wembley. It was jammed into the tower which housed the central heating pipes and services, and

this was a perfect example of the remoteness that the town can provide for high-flying birds.

There are a great number of examples of successful and unsuccessful colonisers of town: on quite small islands, below the crow's nest on the embankment, you can find birds such as the hedge sparrow, the woodpigeon, and the blackbird, all in a sense 'pre-adapted' for town life from an evolutionary past in which they colonised woodland or woodland edge. Whatever species is considered, the questions are the same: what does the animal need, and what has the town got to offer?

There is one comparison of superficially similar creatures that particularly interested us: the frog and the toad. These amphibians must have done very badly while London was being built, for the advance of bricks and mortar was almost always preceded by the draining of the marshland which was their natural habitat. Though both frogs and toads live on dry land for much of the year and hibernate in winter in holes in the ground, they must have shallow water in which to breed. Very early in the spring, they emerge *en masse* from their winter burrows and head for the nearest suitable spot in which to deposit their eggs. The frogs come out first, and their migration is over a slightly longer period and over shorter distances than the toads'.

These migrations are a time of crawling sexual frenzy, with males hijacking females as they make for the water, and attaching themselves to their backs. Toads indulge in the same kind of leap-frog, and the migration is largely confined to a few, warmish wet nights in early spring. So a great problem for both species is to find a pond. It seems that the toad has the harder task. Toads roam over larger areas than frogs, and feed after the breeding season on worms and insects, whereas the frog hangs

around the pond and catches flies at night with its whiplash tongue. In certain areas, the entire population of toads makes for a single, suitable pond in a crawling mass, and if the route is across a busy road, hundreds are wiped out. This kind of massacre, which has attracted a great deal of publicity, probably has little effect, as very large numbers would die anyway, eaten by predators such as crows and herons. What is critical is the scarcity of suitable ponds. Why toads favour only select ponds, while the frog can make do with almost any little lily-pad in suburbia is not understood. But the fact remains that the toad does not find the kind of habitat it needs in town as readily as the frog.

There is, however, a small group of

This marshy ground on Hampstead Heath is rare in towns; frogs and toads have a hard time finding suitable breeding grounds.

spectacularly successful wild creatures which have not colonised the town in the same way as most wildlife in the sense that their association with man goes back far into history. These are the species we mentioned in the first chapter which rely least on city vegetation – the sparrows, pigeons, rats, mice and cockroaches. As colonisers of towns they are in a class of their own, and are often called 'commensal' animals, which means literally, 'sharing the same table as man'. Interestingly, most of these creatures adopted this way of life a very long time ago, with the first civilisations of Asia and the Middle East; and were in a sense 'pre-adapted' to modern urban life.

To provide a contrast with the peace of Buckingham Palace Garden, we

In the sexual frenzy of the breeding season, male frogs clamp themselves onto the backs of females and often 'piggy-back' to the mating pool.

filmed a sequence outside during the Changing of the Guard, and hoped to get some shots of a few urban specialist species living their lives amidst the clicking of cameras and the rum-te-tum of the band. We expected to find the house sparrow, and there he was perched on a gilded wrought iron lion in the middle of one of the gates, chirruping away. What we had not realised was that all of the gates of Buckingham Palace have been occupied by an extensive colony or, to use the conventional term, 'college' of sparrows. Their grass nests are tucked in behind the heraldic detail of the gates, and we watched the parent birds go in and out with food, much of it insects caught in Green Park or St James's Park. Sparrows ignore the crowds below, but if you point a camera at them they become rather nervous, and some very irritating minutes were spent waiting for them to pop in to their nest-holes

down the stone pillars which support the gates.

There were London pigeons too, engaged in a bit of unselfconscious courtship on the gates, the male cooing and blowing out its neck feathers in comic ritual display. We could see the pigeons going in to nest-sites on the Palace, and one was actually building its flimsy twig construction on the cold stone shoulder of Queen Victoria, whose memorial was covered in scaffolding put up by renovators. And there were starlings. For a while we could not see where they were nesting. We watched various likely places. One of us was peering in the direction of the Palace when a starling was seen to land on the paws of a stone lion which sits to the side of the main building. The bird had some insects in its mouth so it was obviously heading for a nest. But the niche it had chosen was quite unexpected: it hopped straight into the lion's

Toads seem to do less well in town than frogs, for their lifestyle forces them to make more hazardous journeys to their breeding ponds.

mouth, and flew out again a few moments later. Seeing this inspired us: what a wonderful sequence would be made of birds nesting in London statues. Was there, somewhere, a lion with not only a hollow mouth, but a hollow at the rear? And a nest in each? And one bird flying in one end, and . . . There might even be a very large carved head, with two enormous hollow ears, and a nest in each?

It is very difficult to take birds like sparrows, pigeons and starlings seriously. They do such oddly endearing things. In the Mall leading up to the Palace, the lamp-posts are topped by iron galleons, and sparrows regularly build their nests in these, perching on the bows like sailors scanning the sea for land. But the real question about the sparrow is why it, of all birds, should be so successful in towns.

The house sparrow is found only where there is human habitation, whether this is a lone farmhouse in the countryside or the centre of a city. Its natural habitat is urban, and the sparrow appears to have adopted this way of life several thousand years ago. It is probably a native of north Africa and the eastern Mediterranean. There are now, spread right across Europe, sever-

House sparrow colonies nest in the wrought ironwork of the gates of Buckingham Palace, where they indulge in some bizarre sexual activities.

al varieties of house sparrow which are thought to represent the historical record of a movement of the bird from its native land westwards.

The sparrow's bill is that of a seed-eater, though like many such birds, it will include insects in its diet. When the first agricultural settlers planted fields of grain they provided seed-eating birds with an exceptionally abundant food supply. Sometimes, too, the birds provided food for the settlers, and 'sparrow pots' were attached to houses to encourage the birds to nest so that the young could be taken and eaten. Buildings, anyway, would mimic the natural nesting-sites of these birds, which build in trees, thatch and in holes. What evidence there is suggests that the sparrow became attached to man with the early agriculturists, and followed him across Europe. If this is the case, then the house sparrow was in London from the beginning and would have prospered as the town expanded. Though the cornfields became more distant from the town as it grew, there was plenty of scattered grain fed to horses and other animals, right up to the last days of the horse-drawn era in the middle of this century.

Some sparrows are tame, and will feed from the hand. But most are wary of man, even if they will come down into the garden for crumbs. Just try to get within grabbing distance of one in an area where hand-feeding is not common, and it will be off. The house sparrow, despite its long association with man, is a genuinely wild bird,

A pair of exotic ducks are given a police escort back to St James's Park.

with a very *risque* social life. Some recent work by a zoologist at the Edward Grey Institute in Oxford revealed some of the secrets of the house sparrow's behaviour. A colony of forty or so birds living in and around a farmhouse were marked with individual coded rings so that the researcher could record who was doing what in the frantic *mêlée* of fights and squabbles. It was discovered that, though sparrows pair off to build a nest and raise their young, quite a bit of philandering goes on. The task of the male is to establish a territory and defend it, and his mate, from interlopers. In any colony there are non-breeding birds looking for a chance to get in, and to mate with someone else's sparrow spouse.

A male sparrow not only has to protect his nest against other males trying to take it over, he has to defend his mate against infidelity as well (it is called 'mate guarding' in zoological jargon and is quite common). However, he will find time now and again for a brief fling himself, mating with other females. This perhaps explains why he will sometimes allow a female other than his mate into the nest to throw out an egg and lay one of her own (this is known as 'egg-dumping', a cuckoo-like activity indulged in by several species, including starlings). We did contemplate filming the sex-life of the sparrow in one of the Soho colonies, but to capture any of this intimate behaviour would have used up our entire resources, and it seemed hardly relevant to the question of why the sparrow is a successful coloniser of towns. It is pleasing, however, to think that such scandalous behaviour goes on in the very gates of Buckingham Palace.

The London pigeon has a rather different history from the sparrow. It is a feral bird – i.e. it has gone wild from captivity – and this is reflected in the very variable colouring of individuals. It is descended from the blue rock dove

and was domesticated thousands of years ago. Over the centuries the wild town birds have escaped from dovecotes to set up their own colonies. Feral pigeons nest on the ledges of buildings which nicely mimic the natural rocky habitat of their ancestors, so the stone fabric of the town suits them very well. They are grain-eaters which peck at bits of bread as if they were tearing seed from a plant.

The starling is a much more recent coloniser of the rocky parts of towns than either the sparrow or the pigeon. Exactly when starlings began to nest in the middle of cities is not clear, but it seems to be the case that they first used towns for roosting. In late summer and autumn, starlings form enormous flocks at the end of each day, and wheel in the air like a swarm of bees before alighting in a squawking mass in a chosen roosting-place.

Starlings perhaps did not so much move in to towns at first as become absorbed by the expansion of the city which encroached on their countryside roosting-sites. In the late nineteenth century, it seems, some starlings nested in the London parks in summer, but went to the countryside for the winter. The first town roosts lasted only until October, when the starlings left. In the 1920s it was thought that the large numbers of starlings which began to roost in central areas were immigrant birds from Europe: several million arrive in England every autumn. But a study in which birds were ringed showed that the London starling roosts were a gathering of birds which fed during the day in the suburbs, up to ten or fifteen miles away.

The starlings which nest in central London use both crevices in buildings and holes in trees. Although, like the starling which raised its young in the lion's mouth outside Buckingham Palace, these birds can occupy the stoniest parts of the city, they almost

The house sparrow's association with man goes back thousands of years; a red hot poker provides a meal of nectar for this male.

certainly need insects to survive. Starlings have a unique method of feeding which you can see if you watch them on the grass of the parks. They plunge their heads down into the grass roots and prise them apart by opening their beaks. This feeding method is referred to by the experts as 'prying' or 'open-bill foraging'. Extra strong muscles can open the bill once it has been forced into the soil and expose food items like leather jackets, the larvae of crane-flies (known to everyone as daddy-long-legs). Starlings will also include pollen, nectar and seeds in their wide-ranging diet.

Fascinating though the few birds species which can survive in the busiest and most barren parts of the city are, they are very few in number. This is also true of the mammals, and only the house mouse and the brown rat can get by without any of the vegetation of the city's green islands.

Rather like the sparrow, the brown rat and the house mouse have a very long association with man, coming from Asia thousands of years ago. It is interesting that, worldwide, the species which adopted this way of life are mostly natives of Asia and the eastern Mediterranean, and the long established ability to exploit human settlements has made them spectacularly successful in other parts of the world. Both sparrows and starlings were introduced to America in the late nineteenth century and from small colonies swept across the States, becoming a serious agricultural pest. Wherever ships stopped off, brown rats disembarked also, often wiping out many vulnerable native animal species on small islands. These urban specialists form a very large part of the crude bulk of wildlife – the bio-mass – in towns. They are numerous and conspicuous and it is not surprising that many people have the impression that they are all that is to be found in the city.

Some quite shy woodland birds, such as the nuthatch, can become quite tame in winter. This one was taken at Kenwood, Hampstead.

Although we found the idea that successful urban species were essentially 'pre-adapted' to exploit the town, we are aware that this is a simplistic argument and there are rival theories. Throughout the history of evolution, some species have become successful and aggressive, expanding their range into new territories, while others have shrunk and become extinct. According to the classic theory, those species we see today are a small minority of survivors, for it is generally reckoned that ninety-five per cent of species that ever lived have become extinct. In recent history, birds such as the starling, the blackbird or the collared dove – a pigeon-like bird – have greatly expanded their range, for reasons nobody understands. They have been so successful because the natural selection of individuals with special characteristics is suitable for the modern environment.

Our 'island' theory could be wrong, and the essential quality of a successful urban coloniser may be that it has evolved to overcome the difficulties of town life. Much journalistic writing on urban wildlife refers vaguely to creatures 'adapting' to the city, and insinuates that the fox or the crow or the magpie in suburbia or the London park has developed characteristics different from its country cousins, which have enabled it to penetrate the town.

One of the essential differences between town and country is the number of people about, and for any creature to tolerate the kind of disturbance there is in London it would have to get used to, or ignore, human beings. It might even actively seek out people because they give it food. So it seems to be plausible that one characteristic which distinguishes the wildlife in towns from that in the countryside is 'tameness', and that

The countryside in the city: a song thrush in Battersea Park.

urban species are those which have become tame. In fact, if you take this argument to its logical conclusion, you might say that anything which has colonised the town is no longer truly wild.

With much wildlife, this explanation can be ruled out straight away; it is irrelevant to plants and insects such as spiders and woodlice. It is also not very helpful with birds such as house martins, swifts and swallows, because they are certainly not tame, even if they do not appear to be worried by people milling about below their nests. These birds are no different in London from the same species which nest under the eaves of farmhouses or in barns. They have simply learned to tolerate or ignore man and have never had any reason to treat him differently.

Nobody would seriously argue that town bats are tamer than country bats. For such creatures, becoming tame does not appear to be a significant factor in their survival in urban areas. But there is a large number of species, particularly of birds, which have only colonised large towns during this century: among them the blackbird, the magpie and the crow. In the countryside these can be shy birds which keep their distance from man. It would have been impossible for them to colonise the town unless they had overcome their fear of man sufficiently to feed and breed in parks and suburban gardens. But how could this have come about?

The question of why wildlife is fearful of man in some areas and not in others is an extremely difficult one to answer. Probably the tamest of all wild animals are those found on uninhabited islands, such as the Galapagos Islands where the birds seem to have no fear of man. In Europe, some species are tame in one area and not in another: the robin, for example, which sits on the handles of garden forks in Britain, is very timid on the Continent. The woodpigeon is

quite tame in London, and yet it is very timid in the country where it is still shot as a pest. However, it lost its tameness during the Second World War when it was hunted, but regained it afterwards. How, in exactly the same species, can you have tame and timid populations, and how did some birds lose their fear of man?

There are two possibilities. One is that young birds, born close to the suburban areas of towns, *learned* not to fear man because they were not hunted, and subsequently nested in suburbia, their offspring learning not to fear man, and so on until they reached the parks in the central areas of town. Each new generation of woodpigeon or blackbird may re-learn lack of fear of man, for the habit of tameness cannot be inherited genetically. However, it is possible that tameness is controlled genetically in another way. In the total population of any birds, or other creatures, there are slight variations in 'character' as there are in the colour of plumage. Some individuals may have a 'gene for tameness', a predisposition not to fear man. In the countryside, where the birds are persecuted, all such individuals would be wiped out. But if they occur close to suburbia, lack of fear of man could be an advantage which would allow them to move into gardens, where they can thrive. This would leave two distinct sub-groups of say, blackbirds – the town birds with a gene for tameness and country birds with a slightly different genetic make-up.

Whether or not tameness is learned or genetically controlled, it is a characteristic which seems to have been only recently acquired by some species. Blackbirds, for example, made their first excursions into town in the 1920s, when semi-detached London was being built, and they would only roost there at night. Magpies did not colonise the centre of London until the 1970s, after centuries of persecution by farmers and gamekeepers in the countryside.

It seems to us that the thorny issue of tameness really does not help to explain why some species are successful in towns and others not. Many wild creatures appear to have the predisposition to become tame, in the sense of being able to feed and breed close to man, yet only some of them have succeeded in towns. It is easy to exaggerate the tameness of wildlife in towns. You cannot easily walk up to a blackbird and catch it by the scruff of the neck; most birds fly away if you get too close. There is a keen ornithologist who catches ducks in Regent's Park with his bare hands, and plucks seagulls out of the air so that he can ring them and record their movements. But quite a number of birds he catches have travelled hundreds or thousands of miles from wild breeding-grounds to winter in the park and are only temporarily tame in London. The tamest or most approachable birds in the world, are those which live on remote islands where man hardly ever goes – they simply have not learned what a danger he is.

So the idea that it is species which have an ability to become tame that are successful in towns does not seem to explain much. Neither do other theories about the relative 'adaptability' of different animals. It is hard to find an example of wildlife in towns which in its feeding or nesting behaviour is radically different from the same species in the countryside. An example often given is the kestrel, the small falcon which is often seen hovering above the town. In rural areas, the kestrel has a mixed diet, including small mammals such as voles and woodmice. In London the kestrel, at least when it is feeding young, lives mostly on sparrows. So it could be argued that this flexibility has enabled the kestrel to move into the centre of cities. However, it is not unusual for rural kestrels to catch small birds, and they often nest on rocky outcrops and cliffs. So there has not been a complete change of behaviour, simply a shift of emphasis. Species which have a range of behaviour in their repertoire are much more likely to be able to cope with changes whether they are an increase in urbanisation or deforestation.

The few studies that have been made to compare the behaviour of town and country populations of wild creatures have found no radical differences at all: merely minor changes. Some of these, such as earlier breeding by birds in the warmer micro-climate of towns, do not appear to explain how or why the birds moved into town in the first place. Odd behaviour, like blue tits pecking through milk bottle-tops to get at the cream, is not relevant, for these birds do well whether they have learned this habit or not.

Nearly all successful animals and plants have some flexibility, a range of responses which allow them to adjust to a changing environment. In Britain, all the birds and mammals have had to find a way of making do with an agricultural landscape which altered the natural begetting of the country. And, by altering the landscape, man has inadvertently favoured some species: farmland, with acres of pastureland and scattered woods is ideal country for some birds, such as starlings, rooks and crows, but not so good for heathland birds such as the nightingale. So the process whereby wildlife has had to make do with a re-ordered landscape has been a long one, and any creatures which have colonised the large towns built since the early nineteenth century did not emerge from a primeval wild wood but from a man-made countryside.

The dynamics of the world in which wildlife colonises the town are much more complex than we have suggested in this chapter. We have, for example, treated the 'green islands' in the city as more or less permanent, when one of the most obvious characteristics of a town is that it is constantly being built and rebuilt. Even relatively stable parks and gardens are re-designed and re-ordered. The urban landscape is essentially unsettled, and though this is a form of 'disturbance' which will inhibit a great deal of wildlife, it can also, in remarkable ways, provide opportunities as new 'islands' appear in the form of derelict land. The rapid colonisation of these brand new ecological 'vacuums' have for a long time had a special fascination for naturalists working in towns.

Starlings are a very successful species in town.

THE BLITZ AND THE BUTTERFLY BUSH

W E FELT that we were really on safari in our exploration of the wastelands of London, on derelict sites, along railway lines, around abandoned power stations, and in the great tracts of abandoned dockland. Wasteland as a haven for urban wildlife is now something of a cliché, and it is an understandably attractive idea that as a great metropolis declines, the wild beasts of the countryside begin to move in to roam the ruins of a once bustling part of town. Sometimes it feels like that, when, on wasteground near Canning Town in the East End, red-legged partridge clatter up from your feet and disappear against a backcloth of ruined factories, warehouses and gas-holders. Whereas parks and gardens feel very much a part of the ordered world of the city, wastelands actually look wild, and give the impression that the town is retreating as nature reasserts herself.

But that is not quite right. Without any economic decline or dereliction in a city, or the constant re-working of the landscape by cranes and bulldozers, there would be plenty of wildlife. The wastelands are not wilder than anywhere else, but are different because in ecological terms they are brand new islands in the city, on which a very rapid process of colonisation has begun. If they were left, they could become woodland, and similar to a settled bit of countryside. But they begin as a barren, treeless, piece of urban tundra – a kind of biological vacuum which attracts a host of plants and other species that cannot survive in wooded areas. Before they have matured, they are built on again, or turned into a tarmac car-park, so they are not only new, but temporary islands. And as one of these islands is covered in concrete, another arises when a building is demolished and the whole process begins again.

This shifting landscape, created by the continual rebuilding of the city might be thought 'unnatural'. If it were, it would probably attract no wildlife at all, for nothing would have the means to take root there. But the natural world is not entirely stable; it includes volcanoes, rivers which periodically flood and wash away their banks; forest fires, the digging up of earth by all kinds of animals which produce fresh soil; and the destruction of parts of forest by pests, which open up the ground to the light. Over millions of years of evolution, this changing element in the landscape has been exploited by a rich variety of plant species and other wildlife which have adapted to a tramp-like existence, setting down roots quickly, then moving on. It is these species, some native, others imported from other parts of the world, which colonise the new islands created be dereliction in the city. Wasteland is wilder than other parts of town only in the sense that the vegetation there is self-seeded, and it is left to develop in its own way.

One of the most thrilling stories in the natural history of London is the greening of the bomb-sites in the City of

Industrial dereliction makes way for wildlife: the dried stalks of giant hogweed silhouetted against the east London skyline.

The most desolate parts of the city have a special attraction for wildlife adapted to rocky landscapes. The flowers of a buddleia bush on the Isle of Dogs attracts a migrant painted lady butterfly from southern Europe and Africa.

The barren, treeless ground of this development site across the Thames from Westminster is ideal for such plants as the pink rosebay willowherb, melliot, clover and the yellow Oxford ragwort.

London after the terrible destruction of the Blitz. Since the Great Fire of London in 1666, the square mile of the City around the newly constructed St Paul's Cathedral had been heavily built up. When buildings were demolished they were soon replaced with bigger, newer, stonier constructions, creating, from a wildlife perspective, the most hostile of environments. Then, between September 1940 and May 1941, the bombers of the German Luftwaffe reduced a large part of the old square mile to rubble. It was not possible to rebuild during the war, and the shells of shattered offices were completely demolished for safety. The rubble was left as it was, and remained wasteground for several years. And there began a remarkable flowering of these bomb-sites, which provided some consolation to Londoners who saw the wounds of the battered city dressed in the pink and yellow of wild flowers which seemed to have risen miraculously from the conflagration.

The speed with which these barren islands were colonised by wild plants excited the interest of botanists, many of whom had never before taken an interest in what covered the ground in towns. Bomb-sites became their hunting-grounds, and a special survey was organised by the London Natural History Society to study their flora and fauna, for in the wake of the plants came insects and birds.

When a new island appears in the city the plants are the first things to get a foothold on the barren treeless soil and they create a habitat for other wildlife. One of the most conspicuous and evocative of these plants is rosebay willowherb, which forms great clumps which turn a beautiful purple-pink when they flower in mid-summer. The bomb-sites provide it with a perfect environment in which to flourish, and rosebay which had grown in scattered patches around the capital in the years before 1939 became one of the com-

monest wild plants in London. But how had it got there?

It is well known that the seeds of many plants can lie dormant in the earth for many years and then suddenly bloom when the ground is disturbed, and a possible theory about the flowering of the bomb-sites was that the Blitz had, in effect cracked the hard crust of the City of London and unleashed this sleeping garden which had been buried for years of development. But this was not what happened. None of the flowers and herbs that apothecaries had collected for their medicines around the City centuries before reappeared. The bomb-site flora were mostly new arrivals in the City, so they had travelled there from outside.

This would certainly have been true of rosebay willowherb though the historical route by which it arrived on the bomb-sites goes back thousands of years. From studies made of pollen preserved in the earth, attempts have been made to discover which plants were growing in Britain many thousands of years ago, which are regarded as 'native' rather than introduced from elsewhere. Rosebay seems to have been native. Its natural habitat was probably open ground, for it likes plenty of sunlight, and this might have been provided by the erosion of river banks by floods, or forest fires which have created clearings in the dense tree cover. Rosebay is often known as 'fireweed' because it tends to spring up wherever the ground has been burned.

You can find rosebay in forest clearings today, but it seems that it is one of those plants whose natural attributes have made it well able to exploit the constantly disturbed landscape created by man. For the plant was rare in the nineteenth century, and was sometimes collected for gardens. In the 1920s and 1930s, a rather bizarre combination of technological change and human fashion gave it a new lease of life. When the arterial roads were built to cope with the rapid increase in the number of motor vehicles they cut through open agricultural land, and motorists would speed along the open highway smoking cigarettes. Drunk with this new freedom they would toss their burning cigarettes into the road verges, starting innumerable fires, providing ideal ground for rosebay willowherb.

There was a healthy growth of the plant around London when the bombs fell and created a much greater conflagration right in the heart of the capital. The ground was prepared. Each rosebay plant produces about 80,000 seeds, each of which is attached to a minute and delicate tuft of hairy strands. In damp weather, these strands are held together by moisture so that the seeds are stuck to the plant. But on dry days, from July to September they fluff out to form a kind of feathery parachute and gentle breezes carry the seeds for long distances.

The seeds are simply broadcast. Most will land in ground already colonised by a variety of plants which have established their position and do not allow in newcomers. Deep in shady woodland or on rich grassland, rosebay withers and dies. But on open ground, particularly if it has been disturbed recently and so has no established residents, it has a chance to get a roothold. The more recently scorched the ground the better, for this presents a kind of ecological vacuum in which there is no competition, and rosebay's dispersal system ensures that it will be one of the first to arrive. Once a seed takes hold, it puts out shoots underground from which other shoots break the surface, so that the plant quickly forms a clump which in turn produces seeds which move on next year in great woolly clouds wafted by the wind to colonise any barren spot available.

All plants have a special mechanism for reproducing themselves: many have windborne seeds; others have sticky seeds which cling to passing animals; some have indestructible seeds which pass through the digestive systems of animals into the ground. The single largest group of plants colonising London's bomb sites in the early years had, like rosebay willowherb, windborne seeds. A careful examination of their reproductive mechanisms showed this, but the most graphic illustration was the discovery that there was a richer growth of new plants on the west side of the City of London — closest to the prevailing winds — than the east side.

The number of plants which turned up on bomb-sites was quite remarkable. In 1939, before the Blitz, London naturalists had identified twenty wild plants or weeds which managed to eke out an existence in the nooks and crannies of the most heavily built-up part of the capital. By the 1950s, they had discovered no less than 269 *new* species growing within the old square mile, all of which had been allowed in by the transformation of buildings into rubble. Only a minority of these new arrivals were classified as plants native to Britain. The majority were species which had been introduced to this country over the centuries, a cosmopolitan flower display rising from the ruins of total war. It is impossible to mention more than a few of them here, for each has an intricate history.

Much of the pink of the overgrown bomb-sites was provided by rosebay willowherb, and much of the yellow by a little flower which has the puzzling name of Oxford ragwort. Like so many 'weeds' that grow in Britain, the native home of this ragwort is in south-eastern Europe. It is especially adapted to the colonisation of volcanic ash — a kind of natural bomb-site — and it was first introduced to the Oxford Botanic Gardens in England in the mid-seventeenth century as a curiosity, having been brought from the slopes of the volcano

Mount Etna. This is how it became known as Oxford ragwort, for it soon sent a few seeds over the walls of the botanic gardens and began to colonise the town. It seems that Oxford ragwort was confined to the town from which it took its name until the middle of the nineteenth century when it began to turn up elsewhere. The records of its spread are scattered, and date from 1833 when it was noted in Berkshire. It seems to have reached north Devon and Worcester in 1835.

Like rosebay willowherb, Oxford ragwort has seeds which are windborne on tiny parachutes, and each plant can produce about 10,000 of these in a year, though some really large specimens can broadcast as many as 164,000 seeds. The official name of this plant – all classifications are in Latin – is *Senecio squalidus* and the uncomplimentary 'squalid' tag refers not to its pretty yellow flowers but to the sort of ground in which it is likely to flourish.

It is generally believed that the coming of the railways helped Oxford ragwort, for the breeze created by the trains swept the seed along, sparks from the engine would set fire to vegetation along the route, and the tracks were supported on a strip of arid clinker which provided the sort of scorched, ecological vacuum which this, and many other plants, found particularly favourable. The Great Western Railway was opened between Oxford and London in 1838, but Oxford ragwort did not arrive in the capital until 1867, so it would seem that it took about thirty years to blow along the line. Once established in the London area, Oxford ragwort was ready for the opportunities offered by the bomb-sites of the Blitz and it was one of the earliest colonisers.

Coltsfoot, also called 'poor man's tobacco', flowers before most plants and grows leaves later in the year. This one was on the proposed route of the new Docklands railway.

Another, taller weed plant with yellow flowers that appears to have benefited from railway buildings and become common on the bomb-sites, is Canadian fleabane. It is thought this plant arrived from North America in the eighteenth century, and first appeared in the London area growing from walls and on bits of wasteland. This is another prolific producer of seeds which travel on small, windborne parachutes.

Many seeds simply blew in to the bomb-sites, but there are other means of transport used by colonisers. The same kind of plant could arrive in several different ways, for its seeds might get caught on the wheels of a vehicle and fall off near a favourable site, they might be eaten by birds and deposited in droppings, or they might be caught in the hairs of animals or the turn-ups of trousers (for such was the fashion in men's wear in the 1940s).

The great expert on weeds, a former director of the Royal Botanic Gardens at Kew and a botanist of the bomb-sites, Sir Edward Salisbury, carried out some experiments on the way in which weed seeds could travel. Sir Edward once raised three hundred plants of twenty different species from one sample from the turn-ups of his trousers! He also grew on specially sterilised soil a sample of seeds gleaned from the mud collected from shoes and trousers around the base of pews in a church and swept outside. From such an unlikely source he raised plantains, daisies and chickweed and similar research has gleaned up to forty-three species of plants which can be grown on from mud.

So quite a few bomb-site plants could have arrived on clothing and on the boots of the City of London's wartime workers. Still more would have been taken there by pigeons and house sparrows. The kind of ecological chain of events which took place on bomb-sites, and continue to operate on wasteground, can be surprisingly and pleasingly complex. For example, many seeds that are eaten by pigeons will survive intact on their journey through the bird's digestive system. Charlock, poppy and plantain are three such plants. It takes a pigeon between half an hour and three hours to digest its food, a period in which it can cover a considerable distance. So a pigeon feeding on wasteground seeds on one side of London, could, in theory, deposit the seeds on the other side of the capital. Where a pigeon is killed by a predator, which in London could be an owl, a kestrel or a crow, before it has fully digested what is in its crop, the number of viable seeds will be much greater. These seeds would not be eaten by the predator and would go into the ground where the victim fell.

House sparrow droppings have also been found to contain many weed seeds, including the very common shepherd's purse, fat hen, ribwort, groundsel and chickweed. Sparrows regularly feed on the weed grain harvest on wasteground in the late summer, and on the bomb-sites, as today, must have been responsible for spreading many plants from one place to the next. To get a place on the bomb-sites, a plant has to be near enough to colonise them, and its ability to do so was often the result of a very long history of transport by man from another part of the world, from where it spread and established a thriving community. Some of the plants found on the bomb-sites had very evocative names suggesting an ancient association with the native wilderness. One was called 'gallant soldiers' or 'soldiers of the queen'. In fact, this plant was from Peru, and had been taken to Kew Gardens as an interesting specimen in 1869. It was given a Latin name *Galinsoga parviflora*, which was soon corrupted to 'gallant soldiers'.

Getting to the bomb-sites was half the battle for colonising plants: surviving there was another. Generally speaking, those plants which are well-equipped to get in early in barren ground suffer more competition from later arrivals. They have a brief hey-day. Mostly, they like plenty of light and do badly in shaded, woodland areas. And in time they are preyed upon by a variety of animals and insects which move in to exploit them. So the flowering of the bomb-sites was not a once-and-for-all event, but the start of a complex process of change which is known technically as 'ecological succession': in time, one set of plants gradually gives way to another.

It would have been a very interesting experiment to retain a bomb-site untouched for a century. By that time, quite mature trees – perhaps silver birch, or willow or sycamore – would have come to dominate it and most of the early colonisers would have gone. Larger trees would provide a habitat for a different range of creatures which could not survive on barren ground such as magpies and jays, woodmice and voles. These in turn might bring in new varieties of plants; jays, for example, habitually bury the acorns of oak trees and do not always find all of this larder when they go to feed on it. They are believed to be important agents in the spread of oak woodland. Would the oak eventually grow on a bomb-site? We simply do not know, because in a town, open land is never left undeveloped for long enough. Sooner or later, the bulldozers move in, and the ground is covered with concrete. The colonising plants move on to new sites where the ground has just been opened up and survive and thrive in a constantly shifting landscape. The bomb-sites were temporary islands and did not sustain their flora and fauna for very long. But in their brief existence they did support more than a colourful collection of plants and flowers.

It has been understood for a long time that particular kinds of plants have an association with particular kinds of bird, animal and insect because all plants contain chemicals which are essentially a defensive armoury against things which might want to eat them. For many creatures these chemicals might act as an effective deterrent – they either instinctively avoid any attempt to eat the plant, or they give it up after the first try, or those that eat it die and become casualties in the evolutionary war. For every plant, however, there is a range of creatures which has evolved a way of overcoming the chemical defence so that these become associated with the plant.

A bomb-site example was the arrival of the elephant hawk moth to feed on one of its food-plants rosebay willowherb. It is the diet of the caterpillar stage of the moth which is particularly critical, for the adult flying moth has a potentially wide range of food. Elephant hawk moths soon found the abundant growth of rosebay on the bomb-sites, and laid their eggs there, producing in the first summers after the Blitz plagues of caterpillars which crawled around the city sometimes to the alarm of Londoners. The ragworts also attracted cinnabar moths, and these were able to use the non-native Oxford ragwort as well as native plants to which they had become acclimatised in their evolutionary history. While we were making the series, the Oxford ragwort growing in the south bank car-parks was eaten to shreds by cinnabar moth caterpillars. So a simple, ecological food chain began to develop. In time, insects which preyed on the caterpillars of moths which were exploiting the plants, began to move in and control the number of moths. In a short time a budding ecosystem subject to very rapid change began to take shape amongst the smallest creatures.

Jays are uncommon on wasteland because of the lack of trees.

Insects are soon attracted to wasteland plants. The elephant hawk moth caterpillar feeds on rosebay willowherb.

The elephant hawk moth is rarely seen, for it flies by night, but there were plagues of its larval caterpillar on the bomb-sites of the Second World War.

These caterpillars can be found in their hundreds on Oxford ragwort growing between paving stones and in car parks. They are the larvae of the cinnabar moth.

One of the wonders of the bomb-sites after the war, and now common in the most desolate parts of town, the beautiful cinnabar moth.

Perhaps the most colourful and conspicuous of these little ecosystems revolved around an extraordinary plant which was given a tremendous boost by the bomb-sites, and is now almost certainly the most successful of all wasteland shrubs in London: *Buddleia davidii*. This is a cane-like plant that in mid-summer produces trunks of pink flowers that resemble in shape and colour the lilac. Its native country is in north-west China where it grows on shingle beds, a naturally disturbed and rocky environment. It is a very attractive plant, and was discovered by a French missionary noted for his work in sending exotic plants back to Europe. He was called Père David (from which the second part of the plant's Latin name is taken) and he dedicated this Chinese shrub to a Bishop Buddle, an English naturalist clergyman who had died long before buddleia arrived in Britain.

A specimen of buddleia was sent to Kew Gardens from Paris in 1896, and it soon became a popular garden plant with the Victorians. One of its chief characteristics was that the trunk-like blossoms were so attractive as a food plant for the butterflies, and it became known as the 'butterfly bush'. Buddleia has windborne seeds which flourish on open, barren ground, and it soon took root on bomb-sites, bringing with it up to twenty species of butterfly.

It is sometimes said that non-native shrubs like buddleia are not beneficial to the ecosystem because few insects have the ability to exploit its foliage. It is another, and unnecessary source of nectar for the butterfly populations of towns, but they cannot lay their eggs on the leaves because their caterpillars cannot eat them. However, some recent research on the plants has revealed that the caterpillars of several kinds of moth can at least feed on it and that it might not be ecologically 'dead' as once thought.

However valueless a Chinese shrub might be to the bomb-site kind of ecosystem it now makes an heroic showing in the most unlikely places in London, sprouting from the tops of buildings, forming a hedge on the tops of walls, and creating thickets on wasteground which might almost be called buddleia forests. The butterfly bush became part of a bomb-site flora and fauna which over the years drew in some quite exotic creatures.

One of these, a small bird called the black redstart, caused great excitement amongst naturalists, but must have

One of the most spectacularly successful wasteland shrubs, the Chinese buddleia, which forms thickets. This one is on the site of the old Broad Street station in the City.

been hardly noticed by the average Londoner. In Europe, this is not a rare bird, and in Holland lives in back gardens rather like our robin. But it has always been rare in England which is on the northern edge of the bird's natural 'range'. It was therefore a great thrill for the naturalists who were exploring the bomb-sites during and just after the war to hear the territorial song of a male black redstart among the ruins left by the Blitz, and to discover that several birds were nesting there.

In England, the black redstart has a peculiar taste for the most barren industrial and wasteland regions, and the first record of the bird breeding in the London region was of a pair which nested from 1926 in one of the buildings which had been put up for the Empire Exhibition held at Wembley in 1924 and 1925. When the Exhibition ended, many buildings were left empty and were soon demolished (the Wembley Stadium is a survivor of the Exhibition). The black redstart chose the Palace of Engineering for its first nest-site in the capital, and pairs bred in Wembley until the war. In 1927 a pair turned up at the Natural History Museum, in 1933 a pair nested in the fully operational Woolwich Arsenal and in 1936 the bird's song was heard around Westminster.

Almost as if they had anticipated the Blitz, the first definite record of breeding in central London was a pair of black redstarts that raised two broods in the precincts of Westminster Abbey in 1940. Four months later, the Blitz began and a whole new territory was opened up for these birds. They nested in the Cripplegate area of the City in 1942 and soon the bomb-sites were to form their favoured hunting-ground in London. They are still around, and we saw them at Broad Street Station in the City while it was being demolished, in Vauxhall, Camden Town and on the South Bank. It is very difficult to spot them unless you recognise the territorial song of the male, which is an insistent twittering, interspersed and often prefaced with a kind of rattle, sometimes described as like the sound of ball-bearings being rubbed together. Once you have spotted the bird, it is yet another job to find the nest. We failed to track one down in London, despite the fact that we had an army of enthusiastic birders looking out for them.

The most humiliating experience was the day one of our spotters called in to the reception at London Weekend Television to say he had seen a pair of these birds just down the road, and they just might be nesting in the derelict Oxo warehouse. We went out with him, leaving the cutting-room, and found the male singing away, but no definite evidence of a nest. The bird was tiny in this landscape of mountainous dereliction, and though nobody has really understood why the black redstart should favour such places, you could imagine it confusing the brickwork faces of the Oxo warehouse with the gorges and cliff-faces which are its natural home in Europe. We watched it springing from its perch on an iron railing or rooftop to catch insects in the air, rather like a flycatcher. The bird moved onto another half-derelict building nearer LWT, and finally arrived at the building of the *City Safari* cutting room, where it sang and caught flies on the roof. It then crossed the road, and performed above the tables of a wine-bar where nobody noticed it – but looked at *us* very strangely as we peered at apparently nothing in the sky.

We did manage to film the bird at its nest in Birmingham, but in the end the only way we could see of getting shots of it feeding its young was to go to Ipswich, where the bird is being studied and the young ringed, so we could be sure of a nest. This turned out to be in an operating cement-works. The young were almost fledged, and were

The most remarkable coloniser of wasteland in London, the little black redstart, which only nests in industrial areas.

Black redstarts nest in old buildings, and feed their chicks on insects.

hopping around on a ledge outside the nest. Everything was carefully set up, with the camera in a make-shift hide at the top of a ladder, and Mike Birkhead ready with his stills camera down below. A fledgling came to beg, the camera rolled waiting for the adult to come in. Then, from nowhere, instead of the parent bird appearing, a kestrel landed on one fledgling, and another appeared to faint with fright. The kestrel then saw the camera and flew off, leaving one bird dead, and the other in a state of severe shock. In any other circumstances, we would have been thrilled to have filmed the kestrel actually making a kill. What was infuriating was that it destroyed this rare little bird before we could get a decent shot of it.

An astonishing, but unwanted, moment – a kestrel has caught one of the black redstart chicks we hoped to film.

The kestrel, which is much better known and more conspicuous than the black redstart, appears to have become more common in London with the opening up of the City after the Blitz. There are early nineteenth-century records of this small hawk nesting on St Paul's Cathedral, and in 1871 a pair nested right at the top of Nelson's column, tucked in by the stonework anchor and cable. How well the kestrel fared in the nineteenth century is unknown. Kestrels often nest in the most inaccessible places high up on buildings so that the only indication that they might have bred and raised young is their behaviour in the spring. By confining themselves to the more mountainous regions of the capital they manage to live a rather secret life.

However, like the black redstart, the kestrel appears to have anticipated the Blitz, for a pair nested in St Paul's School in Hammersmith, in 1931, and among the other pre-war records was that of kestrels probably somewhere in the Houses of Parliament in 1940. A few years after the Blitz, kestrels were seen more frequently in the City and it is a fair assumption that they prospered on the rough hunting grounds of the bomb-sites, feeding chiefly on house sparrows.

A much tinier, and largely unnoticed predator of the bomb-sites was a fascinating spider which is known only by its Latin name *Segestria florentina*. It hunts by hiding in a small hole in a tree

This fearsome spider, called Segestria florentina, *has taken up residence in the walls of Dean's Yard, Westminster.*

or a wall, and spinning around the entrance a circle of trip-wires. When a passing insect touches one of these, *Segestria* pounces from its hole and drags the victim in. This miniature drama must have been played out countless times on bomb-sites which provided the spider with plenty of nooks and crannies in which to build its ambush, and plenty of insect food. Now, we could only find it in Dean's Yard, Westminster.

The wildlife of bomb-sites has a special fascination because it seems so remarkable that anything of interest would live there at all. But, really, it was only the plant life which attained any great degree of variety, as far as we can tell, and it is easy to overstate the interest of the natural world which colonised them. A very large part of the wildlife of the capital, which can be found in the well-wooded parks simply could not survive there at all. In fact, nearly all the characteristic native species of tree, plant, animal and bird did not show up on bomb-sites, for the simple and obvious reasons that the peculiar vegetation which took root there in no way resembled the oak or hornbeam woodland of thousands of years ago, nor the pattern of agricultural field, wood and hedgerow which had for so long provided a semi-natural habitat for them.

What in fact the bomb-site landscape did resemble was the barren, rock-strewn treeless ground that must have covered much of Britain as the glaciers of the last ice age retreated, and before the woodland became established. And that is what wasteground in great cities is like now. It is a kind of rough heathland which is no use for a great range of birds, such as woodpeckers or nuthatches or tree creepers. If left for long enough it might, through the natural regeneration of woodland, provide a place for some sylvan species, but the trees and undergrowth would almost certainly differ from those of ancient woodland because so many of the successful colonising plants would be of foreign origin.

The bomb-sites, and the ever-recurring expanses of wasteground which have superseded them, provide a shifting archipelago of new islands in the urban sea, which arise as a result of economic decline and dereliction, then are submerged again in the concrete tide which washes over them. In the City, extensive rebuilding has wiped out all the bomb-site islands, except one or two which remain as roughly tarmaced car-parks around which remnants of the heroic Blitz flowering, ragworts, willowherbs and buddleia provide a ragged reminder. Black redstarts turn up now and again, and kestrels can be seen around the three tall towers of the new Barbican flats, but both these birds have been on the retreat in the old square mile since the bomb-sites were covered over.

However, many of the new islands that have emerged, particularly to the east in the vast expanses of derelict dockland, have provided a new and in many ways richer hunting-ground for the naturalist with an eye for urban wildlife. Some of these wildernesses came into their own just after the war. One was the old Surrey Docks which were progressively abandoned, and in the 1960s and 1970s attracted a remarkable variety of plants, and birds.

Among the birds which turned up in the Surrey Docks area in the early 1970s, and bred there from 1973, was the little ringed plover. This is an attractive bird with a dark brown and white plumage which makes it almost invisible on its natural nesting-grounds, along the gravel shores of rivers. It makes a piping sound and runs along the ground at tremendous speed, its call giving the impression that it is rushing around in a panic. It was the piping of the plover that led us to a pair on the Isle of Dogs in derelict East London. The little ringed plover is quite common in Europe, but rare in England. The first record of it breeding in the London region was in 1944, at Ashford in Kent. Since then, it has taken to nesting wherever conditions mimic its rather special requirements, if only for a single summer. Like a great many riverside birds, its nest is just a scraped hollow in the ground, the mottled colour of the eggs blending in with the stony surroundings so that they become almost invisible. We watched the plovers on the site in dockland but were unable to find the nest.

The arrival of the little ringed plover in the London area seems to have coincided with the aftermath of the great inter-war road-building schemes and the more widespread use of concrete which left a string of gravel-pits around the capital. A worked-out gravel-pit soon fills with water and is colonised by plants which favour this kind of habitat so that for a time it resembles riverside shingle. By chance, the edges of newly abandoned gravel-pits seem to have taken on the characteristics of the favourite nesting-sites of the little ringed plover.

In much the same way as the constantly reoccurring wasteland of a great metropolis provides conditions which allow opportunist wild flowers to flourish, so the continual creation for short periods of conditions resembling the banks of rivers which are exposed to a fall in water level has suited the little ringed plover. It has nested in the most extraordinary places, including the reservoirs at Walthamstow when they were drained for repairs. Each year, these birds find a place somewhere that appeals to them, and even nest alongside the bulldozers on gravel-pits which are still being worked.

Altogether, there are sufficient nesting-sites for the little ringed plover in the London area for this region to be considered one of its chief strongholds in Britain. It is interesting that this is not a bird like the blue tit or the crow which finds in the relatively fixed conditions of built-up areas – the parks and gardens – the conditions they need to survive and breed. The little migrant plover, like the black redstart, takes advantage of the unsettled nature of the city.

There are other examples of animals with specialised requirements which find here and there in the urban landscape a kind of synthetic replica of their natural habitat. The Surrey Docks site is now almost completely redeveloped with superstores, new factories and housing. But on the north bank of the river, further east, there are wasteland sites which are attracting a quite bizarre range of bird life.

Some of these wastelands are quite extraordinary. There is one enclosed by chemical factories and wharfs where the Barking Creek winds into the Thames at Canning Town, a district which became in the late nineteenth century a by-word for hideous industrial pollution. There is a promontory formed by a loop of the Barking Creek known locally and obscurely as 'The Limo' which is linked to a larger area loosely known as Thames Wharf. Here you will find the pretty sparrow-sized stonechat, a bird associated with heathland and rocky moorland.

The red-legged partridge has also been seen in the summer, which suggests it may be breeding, as has the pheasant. There are quite a large number of partridge a little further east on one of the weirdest landscapes you are likely to see. If you slip through a gap in the wire-fencing of a disused power-station, wade through rubble, rubbish and weeds, you come out into a kind of sunken savannah, and industrial rift valley on which trees and wild plants have grown for years. The underlying 'soil' is a mixture of Victorian rubbish-

The little ringed plover is a rare bird in Britain which does relatively well in London, nesting on gravel pits and wasteland which mimic its natural habitat of river beds.

The red-legged partridge, or 'Frenchman', which has colonised some derelict land in east London.

tips, which collectors mine for old bottles, and the ash-tips of the power-station and an iron foundry. In winter, the quantities of seeds from the plants growing here attract flocks of several hundred linnets, pretty pink-breasted little birds which were once prized by bird-trappers. Goldfinches, which particularly like the seeds of thistles and teasels, also forage here in large numbers.

One of the most remarkable discoveries was the blooming on this over-grown wasteland of two species of orchid. The southern marsh and common spotted orchids are plants which take a long time to get established, and sometimes flower and then disappear. They are certainly not specialist colonisers of barren ground like the rosebay willowherb or the ragworts. But from time to time by chance the right conditions will be created for them to flourish, and this has happened in some

of the most desolate parts of London. In particular, they seem to like the conditions of 'fly-ash' tips left by iron foundries. And there they are, quite surreal, on a piece of wasteland by the Thames in East London.

If you cross the road from this Thameside site, and wander down to the river you find yourself in another man-made, post-glacial landscape. Bits of brick and concrete have been dumped over the years, forming small hummocks which are overgrown with grass and moss and weeds. On top of these you might see the droppings of rabbits, a kestrel cut through the wind and hover above a waterlogged gulley, or in winter you might hear the call of the redshank – a long-legged wading bird – along the muddy shore of the river. It has a moorland feel, but the air is thick with the nasty chemical smell of sulphur dioxide.

Many of these places have been

Orchids are not classic colonisers of wasteland, but flourish where foundry waste gives the soil the right chemical composition. These are marsh orchids on wasteground in east London.

hunting-grounds well known to keen urban naturalists for a long time; places such as old sewage farms attract many birds to their abundant supply of insects, as do derelict canal banks, abandoned water works, sludge lagoons – like those at Rainham in the eastern fringes of London where mud pumped from the Thames to keep the river clear for navigation forms a temporary, man-made marshland – and, of course, railway cuttings and embankments. Each of these provide a different set of conditions which in some way mimics some of the characteristics of a natural habitat. They arise without any thought being given to their significance for wildlife, and are eventually discovered by birdwatchers, butterfly-catchers or botanists on safari in the city; and in the small circle of urban wildlife enthusiasts in the town their names become well known, and they are spoken of with awe, because they often harbour rarities prized by naturalists.

Reservoirs are not like most wastelands, temporary islands in the city, but they have a valuable permanence in the urban landscape. Nevertheless, the kind of habitat they offer wildlife can vary quite markedly over the years, as their use and management changes, or some chance environment event, alters them. A remarkable example of this sort of 'new island' effect on an old reservoir has taken place quite close to the centre of London at Hendon.

The Brent reservoir, or Welsh Harp as it is also called, was formed in 1835 by the damning of the River Brent, and its purpose was not to provide drinking water, but to top up the flow of water in the Grand Union Canal. For this reason, it was not necessary to provide concrete banks at the Welsh Harp and it still has the gentle and muddy shore of a flooded river valley. From its earliest days, the reservoir – which was for a long time in open country beyond the built-up boundaries of London – attracted water birds, including many rarities. But gradually the land around became more developed, particularly in the inter-war years. Industries arose along the River Brent, and from time to time the water was polluted. The reservoir has also been drained at fairly regular intervals for cleaning and repairs. The canals lost their economic importance a very long time ago when the railways arrived, and the canal reservoirs have gradually taken on a new function as pleasure resorts. Brent reservoir has shrunk in size, and is now in two sections connected by a narrow neck. Its banks are still quite wild in places and it has an exceptionally rural feel for a reservoir in such a heavily built-up area, bounded as it is by Wembley Stadium, factories and the vast new shopping centre at Brent Cross.

The remarkable story of the recent changes in the reservoir unfolded in the 1960s. A great deal of new building work, including that on the shopping centre, pushed silt and slurry into the River Brent and began to build up a kind of shallow estuary where the river flowed into the reservoir. At the same time, a mud bank arose from some kind of industrial pollutant which formed the basis of a bed of tall *Fragmites communis* (the Norfolk reed, used in thatching). The reservoir was drained, and during the dry period quite a number of plants became established on the mud and held their ground when the water flowed back in.

These developments have created a superb feeding-ground for wintering waterfowl such as tufted duck, pochard and teal. On the shallow silt beds small crustacea and insects on which many diving ducks feed have increased, and there is now a possibility that the Welsh Harp will become a breeding-ground for birds like the teal. The reed bed has attracted reed warblers, which weave a

Kestrels increased in numbers in central London after the Blitz. They live mainly on sparrows.

nest strung between the stems of the *Fragmites,* and these in turn are host birds to the cuckoo which arrives each spring to seek out one or two species of bird in whose nest it likes to lay its eggs.

A combination of pollution and the draining of the reservoir resulted in a large population of very small fish after re-stocking, and these have proved to be just the right size for a number of birds, notably the great crested grebe. Up to thirty-eight pairs can be found there now, whereas a century ago they were rare. The breeding of grebes, which build a floating nest anchored to a tree or the edge of an island has been helped by the work now going on to provide artificial islands on the reservoir.

An even more exciting recent arrival at Brent has been the common tern, a beautiful little fork-tailed sea-bird which migrates from southern Africa to Europe each year to nest. They too must have benefited from the supply of small fish, but would probably not be able to breed without the help of local naturalists and the wildlife ranger who have provided rafts on which they can nest. It is remarkable to see in this almost entirely artificial landscape with Wembley Stadium in the background, the common tern with its delicate bouncing flight fishing to feed its young.

In winter, the Brent reservoir now attracts enormous flocks of waterfowl which, when disturbed, wheel through

The common tern, which now nests within sight and sound of Wembley Stadium.

This reservoir, the Welsh Harp in north London has been improved as a nature reserve by building developments around. To help things along, artificial rafts provide nesting places for the common tern.

Reed warblers now nest in Norfolk reed which took root on polluted mud at Brent. This pair are feeding a young cuckoo.

the sky and whirr overhead straight-necked in a wild flutter of mechanical wings. Out on the islands of the reservoir, herons sit hunched, their long necks coiled in, and their huge wings wrapped around them as if thrown over their shoulders like a blue-grey poncho. This wintering and breeding-ground for wildfowl and wading birds has been created in part by the silt washed downstream from the building works for the shopping centre, partly by the draining of the reservoir and partly by deliberate help from ecologists and naturalists. It is a new aquatic island, and those who watch the reservoir wait with excitement to see what will turn up there.

If you spend some time watching water birds at a place like Brent reser-voir, or on the lakes in the Royal Parks, it is quite hard to imagine that many of these were idly shot at, often blown from their nests by sportsmen who wandered about with shotguns in London just like the countryside. One of these birds, the great crested grebe, came very close to extinction in the nineteenth century. It is now very common all over the capital from the Round Pond in Kensington Gardens to Brent reservoir, and this shows not only that the conditions have been created in which it can feed and breed, but that it is no longer hunted wherever it appears. So the grebe takes us on to the story of changing attitudes to wild-life, and the importance over the past century that this has had for the colon-isation of the city by many species.

THE HUNTING OF THE GREBE

IT CAME as a surprise to us to discover that some shooting and trapping of wild animals goes on today, even in the centre of London. Crows, grey squirrels and wild rabbits are culled by the keepers in the Royal Parks, magpies' nests are destroyed, the eggs of Canada geese are taken. Foxes are sometimes shot because they have attacked collections of ornamental waterfowl. Out in the wastelands of east London, we several times saw men with guns and dogs hunting and we heard of short-eared owls being killed (illegally) at Rainham. Foxes are dug from their urban earths and their skins sold; badgers are still baited on the outskirts of the city; and men still illegally trap goldfinches, linnets and greenfinches to keep and display as cage-birds. This goes on unknown to most people in London, for those who pursue wildlife in town have to be very careful the general public does not discover them. Nearly all of us like to think of ourselves, often sentimentally and not always realistically, as lovers of wildlife.

Compared to the Victorians, whose approach to nature was as blindly hypocritical as their approach to sex, we are far more concerned to protect wildlife and sensitive to its conservation. Some species would not be around and others would have remained rare, had there not been a move to protect animals from the late nineteenth century onwards. The kind of hunting and trapping that goes on today might be considered cruel or unjustified, but it is not on a scale which threatens the species. The legacy of our former treatment of wildlife, in towns and in the countryside has influenced which species have survived in rural areas, and which had a chance of colonising the city in the twentieth century.

Many species which might have found a place are long gone even from rural areas, or are confined to a few precarious colonies. The last polecat in the London area was shot in Essex in the 1890s. A number of species of bird which survived the nineteenth century took time to recover their numbers, and some have subsequently been successful colonisers of the town. So the legacy of our former treatment of wildlife remains: there are species which can never return without a deliberate effort to reintroduce them; others which have already recovered well; still more which may find their way into the city; and some very successful invaders which are here because of the nineteenth-century vogue for 'acclimatising' plants and animals from other parts of the world to the English landscape and climate in order to replenish the dwindling native wildlife.

There is one bird, the story of which illustrates the significance of a change in the treatment of wildlife better than any other: the great crested grebe. Because it is such a beautiful bird, its behaviour so interesting and it is so easy to watch, the grebe probably gave us more pleasure than any other single creature we studied in London.

If you go at the right time of day, and

the right time of year, you can watch from a bridge across a section of lake in Regent's Park a wildlife scene which is as beautiful and exciting as any in the world. The water is clear and shallow and full of fish, shoals of rudd and roach. Sailing across the water is the great crested grebe, its tufted head held high, with pert arrogance. Then it dives, and you can watch it swim underwater, its webbed feet splayed out, its long neck held forward as it attacks the fish. The bird surfaces, turning the still wriggling fish in its slender beak, then sails towards its mate. The grebes have chicks, odd little creatures with a kind of zebra stripe colouring quite unlike the parents. Often the chicks ride on the back of the parent, tucked in under the wings. The fish is passed by the hunting parent to the parent carrying the chicks. A zebra-striped head pops out from under a wing as the fish is offered, and a chick reaches up and swallows the catch head first. All this you can see from a few feet away.

Surprisingly, few people seem to notice the grebe, perhaps because they do not expect to see it there or to be entertained in such way in a London park. We were able to film some of these scenes without a hide because the birds now have so little fear of man. It was the nineteenth-century fashion for decorating women's hats and dresses with feathers which nearly put an end to the grebe. The rise of a new middle class,

Great crested grebes are now quite common, and parent birds feed the chicks feathers as roughage.

Great crested grebe were once hunted to near extinction because their breast feathers were prized as fashionable decoration.

anxious to deck itself out in finery as inexpensively as possible, started the wholesale slaughter of colourful birds not only in Britain but all over the world. The demand for plumage grew enormously as the century went on, and was subject to sudden fashionable changes chronicled in ladies journals which had been founded to serve the new middle classes.

In the early years of the nineteenth century, the grebe was left alone, and was widely distributed throughout the country. Then, in 1857, fashion caught up with it, and there was a great demand for 'grebe furs', the soft breast feathers which were used to decorate dresses. By 1860, the numbers of grebes had fallen to an estimated forty-two pairs in the whole country. In three years it had become a very rare bird. The decline of the grebe was also hastened by the destruction of its lake and marshland habitat by the rapid building of Victorian towns.

As a rarity in the 1860s, the great crested grebe was given no legal protection. On the contrary, its scarcity made it much more attractive to those ornithologists who were anxious to capture a specimen for their collection before it disappeared altogether. There is a record of such an incident which took place on Brent reservoir in the 1860s. J.E.Harting, a celebrated ornithologist and nature-lover, describes in his book *Birds in Middlesex* an attempt to bag a grebe at Brent. The reservoir was frozen, except for a small patch of clear water where he had spotted the grebe:

On the afternoon of the second day the ice broke up with loud cracks, and, in a strong wind and violent storm of rain, we proceeded in search of the great grebe again. It was with difficulty discovered swimming very low in the water, and showing little more than head and neck, and often times invisible amid the rough waves. As the boat approached within gunshot, and a cartridge sped over the water, the bird, with scarcely an effort, disappeared . . .

For an hour the grebe continued to dive as 'shot after shot was fired'. Finally, as they approached the bird it took to the air, flying across the bows of the boat, but the gun misfired.

Cold and wet and disappointed we turned homewards in the driving rain, and left *Podiceps cristatus* in the enjoyment of the liberty it had so hardly earned.

When we went to Brent reservoir on a cold February day to recreate this scene, the water was frozen over where it was shallow, and there was only a handful of grebes there, for these birds winter on the coast when the weather gets hard. But when we returned in spring, there were more than thirty pairs nesting there, nearly equivalent to the entire grebe population in Britain in 1860. The grebes' recovery has been as spectacular as their former decline, and they are now well established in London and other towns. On Brent reservoir we were able to film their elegant courtship display, in which male and female look almost identical – they dive to the bottom, pick up a piece of weed, then, surfacing, rise up onto their legs, treading the water and dancing towards each other their heads waving. There are many variants of this display, and we often saw the 'pair-bonding' greeting that the birds perform with a chatter and wagging of their raised crests when they meet on the water.

We were able to film the birds not only at Brent, but in Regent's Park, and on the Serpentine, where we saw intriguing and unexpected behaviour. An adult bird would pluck a feather from its breast – the grebe fur of the fashion era – and feed it to a chick which would swallow it in a series of gulps. This is apparently to provide it with roughage. We saw this several times, and filmed it on the Serpentine.

The grebes recovered to their present, healthy population after they were given some protection by law in the 1880s, and the fashion for grebe furs declined from the 1920s. They were helped by the digging of gravel-pits for the construction of housing and roads which when filled with water after building was finished, created a suitable habitat for these birds. Whereas in 1900, there were only three sites in the London area where grebes were known to breed, they can now be found almost everywhere, and we saw them in the winter in dockland swimming amongst the new factory and office buildings on the Isle of Dogs. We even saw a pair on the Thames by London Weekend Television, though they could not breed here. Most pleasing of all, we saw them on the Round Pond in Kensington Gardens, where they have attempted to breed, and imagined them being admired by ladies wearing fur coats as the parent bird feeds a chick one of its breast feathers.

Many other birds were pursued in the nineteenth century for the plumage trade which supplied a mass demand in Europe and in North America. Fashions changed from year to year: sometimes it would be for 'Mercury wings' on hats, using doves, blackbirds, swallows and seabirds; sometimes for dresses edged with swallows wings, or the feathers of herons or kingfishers. As the fashions became more ludicrous in the late nineteenth century, a jaunty 'walking' style of hat included whole birds, small flocks of finches or a single owl staring blankly down from its fashionable perch.

Before some legal protection was provided for birds, and the fashion for sticking feathers in hats began to die out in the early 1900s, a heavy toll must have been taken. And the plumage trade was not the only Victorian craze which put wildlife under pressure; there was a kind of mass consumption of birds, furry animals, plants and insects (especially butterflies) which had not been possible before, and has not been seen since. It was not that attitudes changed very much during the Victorian era; there were strong Biblical foundations for the treatment meted out to wildlife which had been accepted for centuries. In *Genesis* (IX.2-3) you find:

> The fear of you and the dread of you shall be upon every beast of the earth, and upon every fowl of the air, upon all that moveth upon the earth, and upon all the fishes of the sea; into your hands are they delivered. Every moving thing that liveth shall be meat for you.

With the development and much wider ownership of the double-barrelled shotgun and percussion cartridges, and a kind of democratisation of hunting, there was an unprecedented destruction of wildlife. A few, such as the writer Richard Jefferies, deplored the indiscriminate shooting of birds. In an essay in 1885 (in *The Open Air*) he attacked the slaughter which went on along the Thames:

> The moorhens are shot, the kingfishers have been nearly exterminated or driven away from some parts, the once common black-headed bunting is comparatively scarce, and if there is nothing else to shoot at, then the swallows are slaughtered.

Yet, in the same collection of essays, Jefferies waxes lyrical about the single-barrel shotgun he once owned, and how

Goldfinches have become very common in London since bird trapping was outlawed.

it was more fun than the double-barrelled gun. Even nature lovers would take a pot shot at birds. The poet John Keats, who wrote *Ode to a Night-ingale*, recorded in one of his diaries a trip to Hampstead Heath when he shot a tom tit.

Ornithologists, like J.E. Harting, did not sit patiently like the modern 'birder' to spot and record a bird: they tried to shoot it. There was very little interest in animal behaviour; the efforts of both amateur and more academic zoologists went into collecting and classifying species according to their bone structure. For this, you needed a carcass. Harting writes about the time he saw a lesser spotted woodpecker in a tree and promptly went home to get his gun. He waited several hours for the bird to return to where he had seen it, and shot it. '. . . I found it was a female. I waited till dark for the male, but saw nothing of him.' Such patience and dedication

provided quite a bit of information about the anatomy of various species, but did little to help them survive.

Egg and nest collectors, too, made it difficult for many birds to breed, particularly those which were already becoming rare. There are records of people actually drilling holes in trees to extract the eggs from woodpeckers' nests, and a few shillings might be paid to country boys if they could find the nest of a nightingale, or a little bird called the Dartford warbler, which now survives in Europe, but was almost certainly driven to extinction by collectors on the heathlands around London.

As well as the plumage hunters, the ornithologists, and the egg and nest collectors, there were the cage-bird trappers. There is a very colourful group of birds, some of which are now quite common in London, that were trapped on a large scale and kept in cages just as canaries and budgerigars are today. This was a popular pastime amongst eastenders, and in particular the huguenot weavers of Spitalfields, originally protestant refugees from French catholic persecution. Goldfinches, greenfinches, chaffinches, bullfinches, linnets, nightingales and thrushes were all prized for their bright colouring or their song. Singing birds were used for a form of gambling: they were taken in cages to a pub and put on a shelf where they sang 'against' rival birds, the winner being the one that warbled longest. Taking a chaffinch into the country to get it to sing against wild birds, and to keep it in voice for the next competition was also a popular sport. For these purposes, hundreds of thousands of small birds were caught every year with a variety of traps, including bird-lime and mist-nets. Though illegal, this persisted in the 1930s and still goes on today.

The Victorian collectors were after beauty and rarity – in birds, plants and butterflies. The plumage hunters pursued decorative feathers. The cage-bird enthusiasts took pretty finches from the wild. But the Victorian game-keeper was out to destroy almost everything that might conceivably compete with man as a predator of the game birds in his charge. Falcons, hawks, hedgehogs, foxes, otters, pine martens, polecats, jays, crows, magpies – all those species which included in their diet, however occasionally, a pheasant chick or a pheasant egg, were shot and trapped. And the larger predators, because they are at the top of the food chain, and therefore relatively few in number, were particularly vulnerable to persecution.

In the middle ages, when the sport of falconry was popular amongst royalty and the aristocracy, the eries of falcons and hawks were protected. Wild birds provided the fledglings which could be trained to hunt all kinds of prey. There was a hierarchy of hawks: the kestrel was a knave's bird, the tiny hobby which catches insects and swallows in flight was a lady's bird, and the peregrine falcon the man's and the most prized. But this sport mostly died out centuries ago, when falcons were replaced by sporting guns. About the only reminder in London today of its former popularity is the obscure connection with the word 'mews'. When falcons moult after the breeding season they are 'mewing', and the place where the king kept his falcons near the site of Charing Cross was called a mews. This building became in time a stable for the king's horses, so the term 'mews' was applied to all courtyards where horses were stabled, and the grooms lived.

Falcons not only went out of fashion, they were branded as vermin and ruthlessly persecuted by gamekeepers whose job it was to provide as large a population of game-birds as they could for their masters to shoot in massive drives which would produce bags numbered in hundreds or even thousands. Birds of prey were shot on sight, their nests destroyed, and snares set for them all over the estates. Among the targets of the gamekeepers were red kites and buzzards. The kite is a large fork-tailed hawk which is a scavenger in many parts of the world, raiding rubbish-tips and living in towns. It was common in Elizabethan London and was protected, for it was thought useful as a street cleaner. Kites are recorded as pinching washing from the line, stealing bread from children's hands, and flocking around the impaled heads of traitors to pluck out their eyes. Today, the red kite is almost extinct in Britain, with one precarious group surviving in Wales. The more effective double-barrelled shotguns in the nineteenth century made the killing of birds easier, and the scale of gamekeeping and shooting brought the persecution of these birds to a peak.

Like many birds of prey, kestrels were persecuted in the countryside for centuries. A decline in gamekeeping may have helped them recover, and to colonise the town.

The destruction of wildlife in the nineteenth century is akin to that which is condemned today in third world countries, which, as they develop are driving many species to extinction or rarity. It took place at a time when towns were growing rapidly and consuming the countryside around them, when new farming practices were altering the landscape, and forests were disappearing at a great rate. Simultaneously, habitats were being destroyed and dwindling numbers of certain species were being hounded by more people. Not only were the foggy, polluted towns less hospitable to wildlife than they are today, the countryside around was being pillaged on quite a different scale.

A number of wild animals, like the great crested grebe, recovered sufficiently well from persecution to colonise towns as attitudes changed earlier this century. Some legal protection was given to them, or the activities of gamekeepers declined. But, as in the case of the grebe, their ability to make a comeback in town was dependent not simply on a slackening of the activities of the hunter and trapper – the habitat had to be there for them to exploit.

One very successful survivor from the days of widespread bird-trapping is the goldfinch. We saw this brightly coloured little bird on almost every bit of wasteland in London, particularly in the late summer when the young are fledged and quite large flocks feed on the seed heads of teasels, thistles and other scrubby vegetation. It is easy to miss, for its colouring of gold and red and yellow blends with tall weeds, and when it flies you can only tell it from a sparrow by the flash of gold on its wings. Its song, which is like the tinkling of tiny bells, is quite distinctive and can be picked out through the hubbub of the city. Any patch of seeding thistles is worth a glance, as goldfinches are attracted to these however bleak the landscape: in some parts of the country they are known as 'thistle twitters'.

If you see a goldfinch, you will understand why they were trapped by the cage-bird collectors. There is no more colourful little bird in London. Protective legislation, which has outlawed the trapping and sale of wild birds, and the unintentional creation of the kind of terrain they like in the heart of the city on derelict building-sites mean there is a good chance of seeing a goldfinch anywhere in London.

There are other birds, once common around London and favoured by the bird-trappers, which have not returned. One is the nightingale which was prized not for its colouring but for its song. According to the records of the London Natural History Society, this bird has not been near Berkeley Square, or the centre of town, since the turn of the century, except on rare occasions. The last places in which it is reported to have sung in inner London were Portman Square in 1933, Kensington Gardens in 1936, and Campden Hill Place in 1938. Yet it was quite common as a breeding bird in the nineteenth century in Hampstead, Regent's Park, Kensington Gardens, Hackney, Lewisham and Stoke Newington.

The nightingale nests near or on the ground, and it favours areas of low shrub. Its virtual disappearance from the built-up areas of town seems to be due principally to the destruction of breeding-sites. It now only breeds on the rural fringes of London and has never recovered from the depredations of the bird-trappers.

The fortunes of many other birds favoured by the trappers have varied chiefly, it seems, according to the suitability of the town for recolonisation as their numbers recovered. Chaffinches, which have a very pretty, extended song, are not very common in central London, and seem to be losing out to greenfinches. Why this is, nobody appears to know. Linnets are much more successful than one might expect, and appear to have done very well on wastelands, just like goldfinches. We saw large flocks of the pretty, rosy-breasted linnets in East London, and it was here that we first heard that the modern bird-trappers were still operating illegally.

It is not against the law to keep linnets or goldfinches, or any British wild bird, provided they have been bred in captivity. There is a legitimate population of captive birds, which is a relic of the days when trapping was legal. But caged birds, if not inter-bred with wild ones, soon begin to lose their purity of colour, so the temptation to go on trapping is considerable. There is also a lively trade in wild birds, with quite a number exported illegally.

There is something particularly upsetting about seeing a goldfinch or a linnet in a small cage after you have watched them flitting about in the wild. We filmed some captive birds brought to Mitcham Common for a short sequence in the television series by an eastender who has a large collection of these birds. We were shown captive bullfinches, linnets and goldfinches by inspectors from the Royal Society for the Protection of Animals, who were keeping them as evidence against illegal trappers. The techniques for trapping have not changed much since Victorian times. Call-birds are placed in cages to attract wild birds, which are snared either with bird-lime (the tins of this horrible glue are now labelled 'rat-lime') or trapdoors in the call-bird's cage. The captured birds flit about manically, exhibiting the same kind of neurotic, repetitive routines as many zoo animals. Trapping still goes on, but not on a scale which would affect the population of any species.

The birds and mammals which, as a group, have benefited most from the decline in persecution, and have moved in to the relatively safe habitat of the city, are those which were – and still are – killed by gamekeepers and farmers.

One of the most successful birds in the centre of London, the carrion crow. It is shot by park-keepers, because these birds eat ducklings, but it is not persecuted as much as it once was.

The carrion crow, the magpie, the jay, the hedgehog and the fox have long been hunted in the countryside. All, it seems, benefited from the decline in gamekeeping during the two world wars. The crow seems to have been the first of the birds to move in to London, round about the turn of the century when the rooks were disappearing. Since then, its numbers have increased enormously. The jay probably became a suburban bird quite early on, and now does very well, remaining surprisingly inconspicuous despite its very bright colouring. The magpie is the most recent arrival in town: it was thought to have disappeared by 1949, yet by the 1950s it was moving into suburbia. It did not breed in central London until 1971, when a pair raised chicks in Regent's Park.

None of these birds, the crow, magpie and jay, is welcomed in the central parks of London, and none today has any protection in law – they are all vermin. All three are members of the crow family, and will take ducklings and other fledgling birds, destroy their nests and generally infuriate park-keepers who care for ornamental water-fowl. In the Royal Parks, the carrion crows are 'culled' every year – that is, a large number are shot in the early hours of the morning, and some are caught in crow-traps and then disposed of. The idea is not, apparently, to wipe out the birds but simply to keep their numbers down, a pretty hopeless task given their huge population in the capital. Large numbers of crows form flocks in one part of Kensington Gardens, near the Serpentine Gallery, and, if you watch them closely, provide a great deal of amusement. We saw one standing in a deck-chair, hammering with its beak at the green plastic material, mistaking it

A very recent coloniser of central London, the magpie, is one of many species which has benefited from a decline in persecution.

apparently for grass. Others have been known to pull the tails of dogs to get them away from a choice scrap, and we saw one picking up a bone and dropping it, trying to break it to eat the marrow.

Crows have been shot in the Royal Parks since 1949, and there is a notional 'quota' allowed for each park. There is no doubt that crows will eat quite a few ducklings and young moorhens, but whether the shooting has any real effect is less certain, and the job of keeping them down has been made more difficult with the rise in popularity of jogging. Many more amateur athletes are panting round the parks now in the early morning, and the park-keepers are well aware that the public might not be sympathetic to their shooting crows. In Buckingham Palace Garden, the crows are shot on the nest by the police to protect the ducklings. Here is an example of the contradictory attitude towards wildlife that is still prevalent today – we still want to pick and choose which creatures we have around.

Every year, mallard ducks nest in the Buckingham Palace Garden, and when the ducklings are at the waddling stage their mother attempts to lead them out of the gardens to St James's Park, a hazardous journey across one of the busiest road junctions in the capital. When the Palace police see the duck and her brood attempting to leave, they try to round them up, scooping the ducklings into a helmet, then they stop the traffic and allow the duck safe passage to the park. This ritual, we understand, can be embarrassing for young police officers who are aware that when they march into the road outside the Palace and halt the traffic, hundreds of eyes focus on the gates expecting to see perhaps the Queen or a member of the Royal Family emerge. Then, when nothing seems to be happening, expectant motorists and bystanders get a glimpse of a line of ducklings waddling in stately procession past the policeman's boots. All this care is taken to safeguard the mallard, yet, as we will discover, some other wildlife – not just the crows – is not welcomed.

Though the crow and the magpie are still persecuted in London and other cities, they are now well enough established and fitted to the urban landscape to thrive there. It would take a concerted effort to get rid of the magpie. Because of its habit of eating small birds and raiding their nests, the magpie is not liked in many places, and in one Swedish town, Lund, the police – driving black and white cars which seem to mimic the colouring of the bird – shoot as many as they can in a single drive. Here, the park-keepers will destroy the magpies' large, domed nests and harass them into moving.

The red kite is a town bird in continental Europe, and were its numbers to increase in the countryside it might find a place on the rubbish-tips around large cities in Britain. The buzzard too, could probably survive on the rough grasslands of east London's dereliction, and migrant buzzards are sometimes seen there. From time to time such birds as ospreys, the rare fish-eating birds, are seen in towns, stopping for a day over the Serpentine in Hyde Park or at Brent reservoir. For such birds, the town would be a difficult and 'marginal' kind of habitat, and their numbers are small enough for the wilder rural areas to provide better territories for the existing population. But were their numbers to increase greatly, they might, like the crow, move in to town.

The peregrine falcon, too, could survive in towns – pigeons form a large part of its diet – but it is still recovering from heavy persecution during the Second World War and the effect of pesticides in the 1960s. Peregrines were killed during the war because they intercepted carrier pigeons. In the 1950s, pigeon fanciers asked the government to keep the peregrine numbers down because it was said they were taking too many racing birds. An investigation showed that the peregrine was in real trouble because pesticide residues in its prey were causing it to lay eggs with thin shells, which broke before the chicks were ready to hatch and its breeding had been seriously affeced. The peregrine is recovering well, and it may only be a matter of time before it is seen more often in town. What its reception will be is hard to say. There is a story that a peregrine visited St Paul's Cathedral in the 1950s, and began to 'stoop' – that is hunt by diving – on the pigeons there. Outraged members of the public called the police!

One animal which is still persecuted in the countryside, but is usually welcomed in town, is the hedgehog. Gamekeepers destroy them because they sometimes eat the eggs of birds such as the pheasant and, because they can carry foot-and-mouth disease, they are not welcomed by farmers. Though it is doubtful that rural persecution of hedgehogs was ever justified, there is an old superstition, which may have some basis in fact, that hedgehogs suck the milk from cows. Hedgehogs certainly like milk, and many people in suburbia who find they have a hedgehog in their garden, will put out a saucer of milk for them or find the cat's milk has been stolen. An easing up of gamekeeping may have allowed hedgehog numbers to grow so that they extended their range into suburbia, and are now well-established in town. There is a healthy population in Hyde Park and many central areas.

Because they are quite good climbers, hedgehogs are able to move around town fairly easily. The greatest hazard is traffic, and most sightings of this animal are of squashed carcasses on the roads. But this death toll does not seem to be a serious threat to the hedgehog's survival; sufficient animals from each generation remain to occupy most of the available territory in parks and back gardens. It is now thought that there is a greater density of hedgehogs in town than in the countryside, and it is likely that the urban population is independent and self-sufficient, requiring no recolonisation from outside. Hedgehogs may be moving in the opposite direction, from the town to the countryside.

This may also be true for other wild animals which historically came in to town because their rural numbers were rising. Many red foxes are born in suburbia and never see the countryside in their brief lives, which on average last no more than two or three years. Where such colonisation has been successful, wildlife can become independent of the countryside, and the main centres of population from which colonisation of new areas takes place might well be suburban. This could be the case with the magpie, though there is some evidence that its breeding success in town is reduced by the unsatisfactory diet of scraps it often has to rely on when feeding its young.

It is never easy to disentangle cause and effect in the fortunes of a particular species. One bird, long associated with London, with a particularly puzzling history, illustrates the complexity of influences which man's activity can have on wildlife. This is the mute swan which used to be so common in the parks, sailing majestically on the lakes and rivers of towns, and frightening children with its hissing and threatening display made awesome by its enormously powerful wings.

Several hundred years ago, the swans on the Thames in London were something of a tourist attraction. In 1469, the Venetian Ambassador's secretary wrote home to say 'it is a truly beautiful thing to behold one or two

Hedgehogs were once killed in thousands in the countryside because they sometimes eat the eggs of game birds. In town they are usually encouraged, with a dish of milk or catfood.

thousand tame swans upon the River Thames . . .', and there are several other records in the seventeenth century. The odd thing is that these swans were, quite rightly, described as 'tame', and for a long time there has been a dispute about whether the mute swan is really a native British bird or not. It probably was, living in the fenland of East Anglia which is similar to its natural habitat in Europe. But very early on, in perhaps the eleventh century, wild birds were captured as cygnets before they could fly, and were 'farmed' rather like free roaming cattle. Their wings were clipped so that they could not disappear, and they were owned by individuals.

Like the fish, the sturgeon, swans were 'royal', though exactly how and when they came to be owned by the monarch is not clear. This meant that any free flying birds, without a mark on

their beak establishing ownership by an individual, were said to belong to the crown. As a favour to loyal (and always wealthy) subjects, the crown could transfer ownership of swans. There were hundreds of such owners who would keep tabs on their birds each year by 'upping' them – that is rounding up broods which had bred on lakes and rivers, and counting, marking and collecting the cygnets. So, whether the mute swan began as a wild British bird or was an introduced species, by the middle ages nearly all swans were semi-domesticated, or, if they managed to escape 'upping' and to fly free, liable to be taken into ownership.

Swans were prized for their decorative value, and often given as gifts (rather as giant pandas are bandied about to smooth the path of international diplomacy today). But, above all, the value of the swan was as food – it

For a long time, the mute swan did very well in London but it has almost disappeared from the Thames.

This family of swans is tied up not for eating at a royal banquet, but so that researchers can test them for lead poisoning.

was the most expensive and highly regarded meat you could have. In 1274, the City of London fixed the price of an oven-ready swan at three shillings, while a goose was worth five old pennies, a pheasant four old pennies, and a capon twopence halfpenny. Enormous numbers of swans were consumed at royal banquets. At Christmas in 1251, Henry III collected 125 swans for the festivities. Fully grown cygnets were the prized meat. They would be gathered at the 'upping' in July, and taken to be fattened in swan 'pits' so that they would be ready for the table at Christmas.

The economic value of the swan probably ensured its survival during centuries when its natural habitat was disappearing. But, because of the unusual way in which it was kept it never became a domesticated farm animal. Swans are strongly territorial, each pair defending quite a large area, so they were difficult to keep in pens during the breeding season. The business of catching the young, clipping their wings, setting them loose to breed semi-wild, then catching them again at the 'upping', made sense. Other species, such as the greylag goose, native to East Anglia, became extinct in the wild and were turned irreversibly into the domestic farm geese. The wild greylags now in London have been re-introduced.

Very gradually over the centuries, the swan began to lose its value as food, partly because of the importation of the domesticated turkey from North America, and perhaps also because there was more meat available in winter. At one time, nearly all livestock, such as cattle, had to be slaughtered in winter because there was not enough feed for them, but when root-crops for winter feed became available beef could be eaten all the year round. Exactly when the ownership of swans declined is not clear, but over a long period many must have

returned to the wild – they were no longer 'upped' but flew freely around the country, and many more would live to the breeding age of three years as they were not fattened for the pot.

From 1900, there was an explosion in the number of swans on the Thames, and wild birds became established in greater and greater numbers in and around London. They were helped, almost certainly, by the digging of gravel pits in the 1920s, which provided them with a substitute for their fenland habitat. Until the 1960s, the swan population rose steadily, and enormous flocks were often seen on the Thames in dockland, feeding on grain spills from the ships and warehouses. The swan had, some considered, reached the status of a pest, and they were sometimes removed from parks because of their aggressive behaviour.

Then, in the 1960s, something strange began to happen, and it was noticed in the first instance because of the survival in London of the old custom of 'swan-upping'. Whereas swan-keeping had died out long ago nearly everywhere, the City of London, repository of many strange and irrelevant customs, kept the colourful anachronism of swan upping alive. Two city livery companies, the Vintners and the Dyers, still own swans on the Thames, as does the Queen, whose swan-master, Captain Turk, remains in charge of the royal birds. In July, a flotilla of rowing-boats, manned by muscled 'uppers' who have first downed a few gulps of rum and milk, row and swig their way up river, banners flying in pursuit of broods of swans. When a group of cygnets is sighted, a cry of 'Swan up!' rings out and they close in on the brood, capture it, tie the birds' legs behind their backs, establish from beak marks who owns the parent birds, and mark ownership of the cygnets by putting a nick in their beaks.

The survival of this otherwise absurd

procedure, which provided us with our most enjoyable and amusing day's filming, had an important role to play in the survival of mute swans on the Thames in the 1970s. For the swan uppers discovered that there were fewer and fewer birds to mark each year. In central London, the swans virtually disappeared, and the uppers had nothing to 'up' at all. Whereas they had once begun at Blackfriars Bridge in the centre of town, each year they launched their boats further up stream, and by the time we got to film them, they were starting off a long way up-river at Sunbury with little prospect of finding a swan, other than the pub of that name, between there and Staines. On the day we filmed, there were only three broods on that stretch of the river.

After the great increase in its numbers, the swan was clearly in trouble, and though not yet an endangered species was on the way to extinction in the London area. There were many possible causes of this: greater disturbance of nest-sites from pleasure-boats which create a continuous wash along the river banks; the shoring up of the banks; competition from other species such as the Canada goose and so on. A number of swans were also being killed by tackle which anglers left on the banks of the river. The birds would be found, trussed by a hook, line and float which had been thoughtlessly discarded at the end of the day. And some birds had crooked necks, dying maimed by some poison.

The livery companies and the Lord Chamberlain's office funded some research by the Edward Grey Institute in Oxford to find out what was going on, and began a long battle between the conservationists and anglers which is only now being resolved. The researchers discovered that swans were being killed by lead poisoning. Swans feed by sifting through their beaks the mud on the bed of the lakes and rivers – you can see parties of them feeding with their necks extended underwater. Many anglers were throwing away tackle with lead shot attached, and quantities of lead pellets accumulated on the river bed. To grind up their food, swans swallow stones which lodge in their gizzard, and they inadvertently began to swallow lead shot along with the gravel they took in while feeding. The lead is ground up, and goes into their blood stream.

The poisoning affects their nerves and muscles, and produces a weakness which is crippling, so that in time they die. It is a bizarre story, and the angling community have found it hard to accept, but the truth is that having spent centuries preserving swans for the table, then having left them free to

A mute swan caught by angler's tackle. Some swans die from these entanglements, but the real problem is the lead weights the swans swallow.

multiply in the wild, we were killing them off unintentionally.

Swans have not yet recovered in those areas where there is a lot of fishing, but non-toxic alternatives to lead weights, and better river-bank behaviour by fishermen should save them. A great deal of effort has gone into identifying the cause of their decline, and in to cleaning rivers and lakes of fishing tackle. Today the swan, like so much wildlife, is valued not as food but simply for what it is – a beautiful wild bird. One of the most evocative sights in our exploration of changing attitudes towards wildlife was during the filming of the swan-upping on the Thames. When the uppers have caught, trussed and marked the birds, they hand them over to a research team which lays them out on the bank or in their small dinghy, the birds grunting and squeaking. They then take blood samples from them to check the lead levels in their blood, weigh them, and release them again, with feathers ruffled but otherwise unharmed. The uppers row off – or more commonly hitch a ride from a motor-boat – to the next pub, where they eat chicken in a basket or some such food, having, in their colourful and archaic way employed an absurdly outmoded ritual to help solve a very real conservation problem.

There is another, much more familiar bird in London which owes its survival and success in town to the fact that it was once eaten. The London pigeon, which we feed in parks and Trafalgar Square, used to feed us.

We mentioned in Chapter Two that the ancestor of this bird is the blue rock dove. At least six thousand years ago, and probably before, these birds were domesticated and their young, known as squabs, taken as food. It is probable that cave-dwelling men began this practice, sharing their cavernous homes with these cliff-nesting birds. The Romans considered the domesti-

cated rock dove to be a great delicacy and kept them in *columbaria*, pigeon towers, where the birds were force-fed bread which was first chewed by slaves (who would no doubt be astonished to see what goes on in Trafalgar Square). These early 'battery' birds not only had their wings clipped; their legs were broken so that they could not move about. The exceptional homing instinct of the pigeon was also recognised thousands of years ago, and they were used to carry messages at the first Olympic Games in Greece. Later, the Emperor Nero got his racing results by carrier pigeon.

The keeping of pigeons was an art about which a great deal was written, and the Romans probably brought the practice to Britain. Wild blue rock doves survive in the north of Scotland where they live on sea-cliffs, but the first ancestors of the city birds were probably introduced. From Norman times, manor houses all had their dovecotes, in which the birds were kept and their young collected for food to provide fresh meat in the in the winter. Peasants were not allowed dovecotes, and there is a nice description in one of Walter Scott's historical novels of the neat way in which the laird robbed the villagers of their corn by allowing his doves to raid the peasants fields so that he could eat the fattened bird.

As a source of food, domesticated pigeons lost their value once cattle could be kept through the winter, and birds began to go wild as dovecotes were abandoned. They had lost their true, wild colouring however, and colonised towns as a motley crew, or found blue rock dove colonies which they rejoined. But pigeons continued to be kept as messengers, and by breeders who turned them, by artifical selection, into a grotesque collection of freaks, with feathery feet or great, pouting throats.

Carrier pigeons were used by the

British Army in both the World Wars, and in 1944 a bird called Winkie won a medal for carrying a message from a plane that had crashed in the North Sea back to HQ. Pigeons were parachuted into occupied France to carry out messages from the resistance movement, bringing them back to Oxford Street. There are commemorative monuments to them in Brussels and Lille. On the whole, carrier and racing pigeons are very reliable, but bad weather and exhaustion can make them stray to the wrong town. So the stock of feral pigeons is always being replenished and you can see ringed racing pigeons in Trafalgar Square enjoying a new life posing on the heads of tourists. Pigeons are now doing very well, and in some districts where counts have been made, seem to have dislodged the house sparrow as the dominant species. But they are largely dependent on human largesse for their survival, and when a law prohibited the feeding of them while rationing was in force during the Second World War their numbers reduced. They now have an ambiguous status, for while half the population feeds them, the other half is trying to get rid of them because their droppings deface and erode buildings and they are a serious pest where food is stored in warehouses.

The desire to manipulate wildlife, to pick and choose what should survive and what should be eliminated, remains very strong, but it has been tempered by a greater understanding of the ecological impact of messing about with nature than existed in the nineteenth century or before. And some of the most familiar wildlife in London and other towns today is there because

The London pigeon was introduced to town because it was once thought good to eat.

in the past people thought nothing of introducing alien species to this country to provide something new to shoot at, to feed on, to amuse them or merely to see if it could survive. One of the purposes of the Zoological Society of London, at its foundation in 1826, was to introduce 'new and useful' animals to Britain.

The British shipped out their sparrows, goldfinches, thrushes, deer and trout to the colonies, to make themselves feel at home in foreign parts and to provide themselves with sport. They shipped back all kinds of birds and beast in the hope that they might flesh out the rather impoverished wildlife in Britain, and provide interest, amusement and meat. Most introductions of alien species at home and abroad were a failure, and the pioneer colonies quickly died out for want of some essential ingredient in their diet or habitat. But a few were spectacularly successful. The rabbit, for example, which probably first came to England with the Romans (it is a native of southern Spain and Morocco) was taken to Australia where it multiplied to plague proportions. And the American grey squirrel, first introduced to Britain in 1876 by a landowner in Cheshire, was by the 1930s considered to be a very serious pest by park-keepers and foresters, and efforts were made to stamp it out.

From the late nineteenth century to 1929 grey squirrels were introduced into estates and parks, often by Americans, but for what reason it is hard to tell. In America, the grey squirrel is hunted, eaten, and protected by a close season, so perhaps there was the idea that they would provide a new form of game. Between 1905 and 1907, grey squirrels brought from Woburn Abbey were released by the Zoological Society and allowed to hop off into Regent's Park where they became well established. They spread to all the London parks within a few years and began to turn up in the central squares of town.

At the turn of the century, the native red squirrel was established in the London area, and the simultaneous success of the grey and the rapid decline of the red seemed to indicate that the newcomer had driven the native out. Grey squirrels are larger than red squirrels, so this appears to make some sense, but it is still not clear what happened.

The red squirrel does best in coniferous forests, and London parks were not that well suited to it. In Britain they are on the edge of their 'range', which extends across Europe, and like most fringe colonies of animals are vulnerable to extinction. At the turn of the century the red squirrels were hit by a virus disease which greatly reduced their numbers, and it was at this time that the greys were introduced – though there is no indication that the American variety was brought in as a substitute. Red and grey squirrels did live alongside each other for some years, up to the Second World War, but in time the red became extinct in the London area, to everyone's chagrin, while efforts were made to exterminate the grey, which eats the shoots of growing trees, digs up park-keepers' flower bulbs and strips the bark from trees.

It is reckoned that between 1917 and 1937, 4,000 grey squirrels were shot in Kew Gardens. In 1930, the Royal Parks tried to wipe them out: 2,100 were shot in Richmond Park between 1932 and 1937. Between 1945 and 1955, a bounty of one shilling a tail was paid for grey squirrels in rural areas, and free cartridges were given to squirrel shooting clubs. But the grey has survived, and has now so endeared itself to the public in the parks of London and other cities as a kind of semi-tame animal that attempts to control its numbers have become more difficult.

Grey squirrels are still trapped and

shot in the Royal Parks, but the practice was considered to be so sensitive we were not allowed to film it. The park-keepers go out in the early morning when few people are about. There is much more shooting going on in the parks and gardens of London than most people realise, but all these efforts seemed to us to be futile, and not to threaten any species at all.

The aim no longer seems to be to wipe out species altogether – though some would like to – while there is great caution about introducing any new creature which might by chance be very successful and turn into a pest. There

has been only one planned introduction of an animal to London in recent years, and that has been the attempt to re-establish the red squirrel in Regent's Park. This is in part a research project of the Zoological Society, involving a careful study of how red and grey squirrels get on together.

One of the strangest sights in Regent's Park where we were doing our research was not the red squirrel itself – which was rarely seen – but the Norwegian researcher David Moltu, who looks rather like Bob Dylan, wandering about holding what appeared to be a television aerial over his head. This

Like a number of very special town species, the grey squirrel was introduced to London. But this North American animal is considered a pest, and its numbers are controlled by culling.

The native red squirrel disappeared from London after the last war, but a few have been brought back in an experiment to see if they can survive. They are fitted with radio transmitters so they can be tracked by scientists.

picked up the signal from small transmitters attached to the red squirrels' necks, and in this way Moltu attempted to check their whereabouts and well-being. Only ten, young, wild red squirrels, brought down from the Scottish pine forests, where the Forestry Commission shoots them as pests, were released in London. They were put first in an acclimatising cage in the zoo – the same enclosure, apparently used for grey squirrels earlier in the century – and then allowed to find their own way out.

Everything has been done to help them. Special feeding-boxes which the grey squirrels cannot use because of a weight-triggered pedal, have been attached to a number of trees. But the red squirrel was clearly going to have a hard job surviving. Within a few weeks of their release, the traces of one – including the transmitter – were found where it had evidently been caught and eaten by a feral cat. Others have been run over, as are many young grey squirrels around the park. There is a pair of red squirrels in the zoo which Moltu hopes might breed: these are 'tame' in the sense that they have no fear of man. In fact, man has a fear of them, for in a brief visit the more forward of these tree rats bit every member of the camera crew, dug cigarette packets out of pockets and proceeded to chew its way through twenty Silk Cut. That is the kind of behaviour which could get it going again in London, and eventually it might compete with those grey squirrels which have taken to 'mugging' innocent passers-by by running up their legs and sticking their noses into a bag or pocket in search of sandwiches.

To date, the grey squirrel is probably the most successful of introduced species from the heyday of 'acclimatisation'. But there are others which are doing well. You will often hear in London, a strange whirring of wings as if some craft from outer space were about to land, and a wild honking

A tame red squirrel kept in London Zoo getting in on the action.

sound, and rush to the window to see a skene of geese flying in formation over the rooftops. These are Canada geese, which, as their name implies, are not native to this country but to North America. The very large population of these birds in town is now entirely descended from introduced pairs.

Three hundred years ago, Canada geese were kept rather like swans, and prized as something to look at, to shoot at and to eat. One of the nineteenth-century gentry naturalists wrote of 'the fine proportions of this stately foreigner, its voice and flavour of its flesh are strong inducement for us all to hope that e're long it will become a naturalised bird throughout the whole of Great Britain.' This has not quite happened, because Canada geese seem to be confined to a number of very healthy but isolated communities in Britain. Unlike their American ancestors, they do not migrate, except for short distances.

Canada geese were kept in St James's Park in the seventeenth century, where the diarist John Evelyn wrote of 'numerous flocks of severall sorts of ordinary and extraordinary wild fowle, which for being so neere so great a citty, and among such a concourse of soldiers and people, is a singular and diverting thing.' But it was not until after the Second World War that they really became established as wild birds in the city, and the story of their introduction is extraordinary.

In the 1950s, Canada geese had done very well in the countryside, so well that they became an agricultural pest as they eat the shoots of wheat and newly sown grass. As a solution to the problem, the Wildfowl Trust and the Wildfowlers Association took more than 1,000 birds from their colonies in rural areas, and redistributed them. In

Another North American introduction, the Canada goose, which keeps its goslings in a communal crèche.

Canada geese goslings: these birds are so successful in London parks, keepers try to reduce their numbers.

1955, Canada geese were released in Hyde Park and Kensington Gardens. The effect of this control measure was to greatly increase the bird's range, for they did well everywhere.

One of the most extraordinary sights now is a massive armada of Canada geese on the lake in Battersea Park, with a group of adult birds sailing in protective convoy around a swarm of squeaking orange goslings of various ages. Canada geese, like quite a number of other birds, operate a creching system, whereby the young are cared for collectively, and this seems to be a very successful form of behaviour in the parks. We saw it in action when a dog off the lead approached a group in Battersea Park. As if they were one body, the goslings which had been scattered ran together into a huddle, while the very aggressive, honking and hissing adult saw the dog and its owner off.

But Canada geese are seen as a pest by many park-keepers, because they rip the grass up and take over territories reserved for ornamental waterfowl. In Hyde Park, the eggs of Canada geese are taken, and the contrast in early summer with Battersea Park is very striking. In the one, there are dozens of geese and no chicks, in the other, a mass of orange chicks easily outnumbering the adults. Canada geese have also become unwelcome guests in Buckingham Palace Garden, where there are plenty of geese but no chicks. Although Canada geese have bred in this central London wildlife haven, nowadays, their eggs are taken in an effort to discourage them.

The habit of keeping non-native waterfowl in the London parks as decoration has led to persecution of other forms of wildlife, such as Canada geese, crows and magpies, and foxes which have been pursued to protect ornamental birds. Yet, the sight of ducks on a lake seems to act as a decoy to other birds, and from time to time a non-native bird which is not pinioned will take off and become a free flier established in the wild.

The most striking of these escapees in recent years has been the Mandarin duck, which is native to China, where its ancestral home is along well-wooded river banks. It is thought seventeenth-century English merchants gave the duck its new English name, after the Chinese government officials, the mandarins. The male has fantastic plumage, as if it had been hand-painted, and the bird has inspired artists for centuries. In Asia, it is a symbol of love and fidelity, for the ducks mate for life.

Many attempts have been made to get the birds to breed in this country, which has a suitable climate, but not much of the right kind of habitat. The first successful attempt was in London Zoo in 1834. Since then, free-flying birds have been released on several occasions from Buckingham Palace Garden, and the central parks. They eventually became established in the wild along the rivers to the south-west of London, and now one or two have turned up in central London. In 1985, those in Regent's Park were actually wild, not ornamental park birds.

The mandarin is essentially a tree duck. It often sits in trees, and nests in holes in old oaks. Its food changes with the seasons, and in the autumn it seeks out acorns, which are possibly a critical factor in its diet, so oak woods are needed for it to survive and spread. In China, it is still kept as a tame bird, but the wild population was almost wiped out by forest clearances – it has never been hunted in the East – and a few years ago it was thought possible that the wild mandarin duck was more common in England than in China.

So many wildfowl do well now in cities, colonising rivers, ponds and lakes, that it is arguable that the keeping of pinioned birds is really an

Once just a curiosity, the Chinese mandarin duck now breeds in the wild in London, favouring areas with oak trees.

anachronism. Often the numbers of birds on park ponds is far too high, and large numbers die from diseases. It might be much more exciting and more pleasing simply to keep the lakes clean and well-stocked with fish and wait to see what turns up. Every winter, ducks such as the pochard and tufted fly from as far away as Eastern Europe to places like St James's Park, and some stay in the spring to breed.

Another introduction from Asia is the tiny muntjac deer, from eastern China, which has escaped from country estates during this century and colonised a large part of south-east England. It is a little bigger than a fox, and lives in low-growing shrubs and woodland, moving swiftly and silently through brambles, rhododendron bushes and the like. It feeds on blackberries, leaves and fruits. The muntjac is now so common on the outskirts of London that some gardeners who have found their shrubs chewed to pieces, consider it a pest. So far, it has not got very far in London, though there is one

record of muntjac being run over near Hampstead Heath, and one was found trapped by a garden fence near Kingston. They are certainly established and breeding at Trent Park near Cockfosters in North London.

Muntjac are small and secretive enough to get quite a long way in to town, at least in to the wilder parks such as Wimbledon Common and Hampstead Heath, though the central parks have too little cover. Rather like a fox, they could get established without anybody noticing them, for they move around and feed chiefly at night, and give themselves away only by a loud, insistent barking which could easily be mistaken for that of a dog.

It is unlikely that any new species of wild animal will be deliberately introduced to this country in the future, either to rural areas or the towns, as the possibility of unforeseen and unwanted ecological consequences is much better recognised than it was. But the effects of the legacy of past manipulation of wildlife have still to be felt, and the

The tiny muntjac deer from Asia has escaped from zoos and now breeds in the wild. It is small and secretive enough to move right into the centre of London.

interaction of all those species which are recovering from past persecution or have gone wild after being introduced will be very complex.

How will muntjacs get on with foxes, and foxes with Canada geese, and Canada geese with mandarin ducks? They may all remain independent of each other, in separate niches, or one may drive out the other. And, as wild-life continues to flow into our cities, it is not clear how the comparatively sympathetic suburban population will react. We found people who were very much opposed to foxes in their back garden. They did not like the droppings on the lawn, the trampling of flowers, particularly by the cubs when they play outside the earth, the possible danger to their pets, or the risks of rabies spreading to this country. So far, opinions have not hardened, and though pest-control officers in the South London boroughs are frequently called in to get rid of foxes, most people are not sufficiently aware of the animals' presence, or affected by it, to worry.

Most people still like to pick and choose the wildlife they have around them. They will spray the roses to kill greenfly, which are an important food for blue tits which come to bird-tables in the winter. Nobody likes slugs and snails, but they are happy to see a blackbird on the lawn. People still kill the worms in their lawn because the 'casts' spoil the smooth carpet of grass. Yet they do not tolerate animals which eat worms, because they create bigger lumps with their burrowing. It may well be that the mole is rare in London, not because it cannot cross the concrete maze of roads, but because it is not tolerated by gardeners.

Many suburbanites dislike 'aggressive' birds, such as starlings, magpies and jays, and would probably have them removed if they could to protect the pretty little species such as the blue tit and the greenfinch. Much urban wildlife is treated as if it were not truly wild, but a pet, and you often hear people refer to 'my blue tit' as if they could tell one from another. An interesting research project in fact revealed that these personalised birds are different almost every day, for garden species are on the move most of the year.

Nailing up a nest-box does encourage many more birds to breed, particularly in areas where natural holes in old trees are scarce. But this is likely to lead to a great slaughter of young in the early summer, with pet cats as one of the chief predators. The nest-box which attracted the blue tits whose young were eaten by the family cat is a frequently enacted suburban tragedy, as people continue to sentimentalise the natural world.

So the conflicts are not all over. What has changed radically, since the first protective legislation was introduced in 1869 to stop the slaughter of sea-birds, is the mindless persecution of almost everything that moves. It is really unthinkable now that anyone would turn out with a shotgun in a London park to take a pot-shot at a rare bird – it is not only illegal, it would be considered immoral. W.H. Hudson, the great nineteenth-century writer on London's wildlife, recorded an incident in 1895, when a skylark turned up and sang all day in Victoria Park:

It attracted a good deal of attention, and all the Hackney Marsh sportsmen who possessed guns, were fired with the desire to shoot it. Every Sunday morning some of them would get into the field to watch their chance to fire at the bird as it rose or returned to the ground.

The skylark got away, but it was not to survive long in central London, for it is a bird which nests on the ground and

For centuries, the wildlife in and around London has been exploited by man: swan-upping has survived from the days when these birds provided a tasty meal.

needs a kind of scrubby grassland to breed. It is still considered a pest by some farmers, but it has found a new and unexpected territory on some of the wildest and least frequented wastes on the outskirts of London.

There has been a radical change in attitudes, which has made the town a safer place than much of the country side for most wildlife today. But it is wrong to imagine that because we appreciate wild creatures more than in the past, that there are no conflicts between wildlife and people in our cities.

SEAGULLS AND SALMON

TWENTY YEARS AGO, the River Thames was pronounced more or less biologically dead for forty-three miles of its course from Kew Bridge to Gravesend. Today, you can fish for dace and many other river species outside the Houses of Parliament. The river is so clean that eels caught by Tower Bridge can be sold in the market, and fetch a very good price. In many ways, our cities have been transformed in recent years: the air is now free of smog and coal dust, and on a clear day you can see for miles. Cleaner air allows in more sunlight, so that a greater variety of plants can grow there, and many more insects can survive in the heart of the city. Because there are more insects, there are many more insect-eating birds, such as the beautiful long-tailed tit which now breeds in Battersea Park and Hyde Park.

If the River Thames were to become seriously polluted again, or the smogs to return, there is now wildlife in the capital which is sensitive to such changes and would die. The first fish to be killed in the river, and to float belly up past the Houses of Parliament, would probably be the salmon, which has returned to the river in small numbers but cannot tolerate low levels of dissolved oxygen in the water and is vulnerable to pollution. Foul air would probably drive out such insectivorous birds as the house martin, the swift and the flycatcher from the central parks. So wildlife might be a kind of 'canary'

in the city, warning us by its death or disappearance of serious pollution problems.

We thought about this proposition a great deal: that a cleaner city benefits both the people that live in it and the wildlife, and that what is good for one is good for the other. While we were researching the project, a number of articles were published on urban wildlife which seemed to take this approach. The 'return' of wildlife to towns was an indication that they were better places for people to live in as well.

This idea directly contradicts another popular notion, that the return of wildlife is a sign of the decline of the city, as its old industrial areas are turned into wastelands. Both views, however attractive they may seem, make the error of assuming that wildlife 'likes' nice, clean places that are like the countryside, or places that look 'wild'. The truth is that wildlife does not care what places look like, none of it has human emotions, and a great deal of it would do much better if our cities were one large, revolting rubbish tip.

Our conclusion was that you cannot equate the well-being of people in a city with the well-being of wildlife — the interests of each are too often in conflict. With every milestone on the course of human progress, from the invention of such nineteenth-century luxuries as the flush toilet, through to the generation of electricity and the advent of cheap air travel, there have been unexpected and often bizarre eco-

Seagulls thrive on London's vast rubbish tips, like this one at Rainham.

The Thames, stinking and polluted after the last war, is now so clean the eel fishermen are back setting their nets by Tower Bridge.

logical consequences which have kept man and wildlife in the city in a perpetual state of concorde and conflict.

Seagulls provide a very good example of this. As far as one can tell from historical records, seagulls did not often come up the River Thames before the 1880s, when a series of cold winters drove them inland. When they first arrived, they were shot at from the Embankment, but the local magistrates put an end to that, and very soon people were feeding them with fish scraps brought from Billingsgate Market. From the late nineteenth century, seagulls have been constant winter visitors to the capital, and to other cities, and their numbers have grown enormously this century. From our office window, high above the Thames, we watched the gulls from mid-summer until late spring, soaring above the Houses of Parliament, and sailing along the river in large flocks.

There are five species of gull commonly found in London, mostly outside the brief breeding season of May to August, and you have to be quite a good bird spotter to tell them all apart, and to recognise them in their winter plumage. Black-headed gulls – which lose most of their very dark brown head feathers outside the breeding season – are most often seen along the Thames and in the parks. There are also common gulls, which are not that common, and lesser black-backed, and great black-backed gulls. The last of these is an enormous bird and, the upper parts of its wings are very dark grey. When they soar above the centre of town, they look almost like eagles or vultures. Finally, there are the herring gulls, the only species which attempts to breed in London, and the sort which makes the characteristic crying and honking sound of the seaside.

Throughout this century, the population of gulls in Europe has risen enormously, chiefly, it is thought, be-cause man has unintentionally provided winter feed and shelter in his efforts to improve his own environment. There are many more playing fields in London for sportsmen than there used to be, and the short turf provides many gulls with both a 'standing ground' which is open and therefore gives them a good view of any predators, and allows them to feed on worms and other invertebrates. The reservoirs created to provide fresh water have given the gulls a place to bathe and roost at night. And, above all, the enormous increase in rubbish, transported to large, open tips has provided the birds with a place to scavenge, and they have for years followed the bulldozers on the rubbish tips just as they follow the plough in the country. One of the most unusual sights we saw during our research was the great pillow bursts of clean white gulls in their thousands fluttering and circling above rubbish tips while bulldozers flattened the garbage, scrunching up piles of nudey magazines, computer print-outs, invitations to weddings and foreign embassies, accounts, love letters and occasionally what looked like something the gulls might actually eat, for there was very little food that we could see.

Seagulls are now the great scavengers of the city, taking over the niche occupied by kites, ravens and buzzards in Elizabethan times. They are very pleasing to watch, because all the species are, in their own way, wonderful fliers, diving and darting, and catching bread in mid-air if you throw it up to them. But seagulls are also a problem. Rubbish tips attract scavenging animals, including foxes, crows, rats and the rubbish, and possible disease, gets scatterd about; if there is a wind blowing it produces an unsightly mess over a wide area. Seagulls appear to bring a special hazard because they will feed on rubbish by day, and then roost in the fresh drinking water reservoirs at night. In London, this has not been a serious concern, because the water from the open reservoirs is purified before it is stored in covered tanks, so whatever pollution the gulls bring should be eliminated. But in other towns, such as Glasgow, where pure water is piped into storage reservoirs from Loch Katrine in the Trossach hills some thirty miles away, the water is simply treated and sent direct to the consumer. Once large concentrations of gulls built up on the reservoirs there was a potential problem which would have cost millions to solve by building a new treatment works and covered sewage tanks. However, a concerted effort was made to scare off the gulls by regularly playing distress calls as the birds arrived to roost each evening. Temporarily at least, this seems to have worked and the gulls now roost on Loch Lomond or the Clyde estuary.

Seagulls have become a real headache in the capital, and anywhere there is an airport. If a jet aircraft hits a flock of birds – a 'bird-strike' as it is called – it can be seriously damaged in a number of ways. A large bird might cause a dent in the fuselage, or crack the cockpit windows. That is not very serious. But if just one large bird is sucked into the front of a jet engine, the plane might lose power and crash, as has happened on rare occasions. All kinds of birds have been involved in these mid-air collisions: lapwings, golden plover, kestrels, starlings, but the most common species to collide with aircraft are the seagulls. Because the seagulls had become a problem, a study of their numbers and movements was set up in the 1950s. The London gull study group is still in operation, and a very strange sight it is when it goes in to action on a rubbish tip.

Through a firm called Cleanaway, which has the contract to dispose of much of the capital's rubbish, we got in touch with an ecologist Phil Shaw, who is employed by them to study the impact of refuse disposal (as they prefer to call it) on wildlife, and vice versa. Phil Shaw put us in touch with one of the few people who has a licence from the British Trust for Ornithology to net large numbers of gulls, ring them, measure them, weigh them and make returns to the gull study group. The gulls are caught with a cannon net, which as its name implies, is set in place and then fired with rockets over the gulls, so they can be packed into sacks and subjected to a rapid process of recording and analysis.

We thought this might be a difficult episode to film, because sometimes it takes hours for the gulls to settle in the area where the net has been set up. So we went along to have a look at how it was done, way out of London on a rubbish tip at Pitsea in Essex. It was a Saturday, and the cannon-netter, a doctor from the south coast, and his two daughters arrived early in the morning, full of enthusiasm and loaded with the most extraordinary collection of gear. All of us, Dr Barry Watson, his daughters, the ecologist and several helpers, got into one small landrover and set off over the wastes of this vast rubbish tip. Crammed in with us were boxes of mouldy bread and fish heads, which stank horribly, and seemed to be quite unnecessary in this pungent landscape created from millions of dustbins. The net was set out on the tip, and we watched incredulously as the mouldy bread and fish heads were strewn in front of the net. Few gulls were to be seen. Though the birds are not concerned about the machines which dump and spread the rubbish, they disappear as soon as any human beings emerge to walk around – mechanical things are not a threat, people are.

We drove away, and took up a position a long way from the net, to watch with binoculars, and to listen to

tales of how many gulls had been netted in one go on other occasions. The sky remained empty. A hen-harrier appeared, and caused a flutter of excitement as it cruised, silver grey over the ground. We continued to wait, but no gulls. The tip was not working because it was a Saturday, and it was apparent that the seagulls did not bother to turn up unless there was a bulldozer there – they had learned when fresh rubbish was being tipped, and knew that Saturday was no good. We got no gulls that day, but we thought it worth a try at another tip, right on the eastern edge of London's built up area at Rainham.

On the day we arrived with the film crew there was a thick mist, and we could see very little, though flocks of gulls floated silently in and out of the gloom. The net was set out, with a hide at one end. In this tiny canvas shelter was the cameraman, the doctor and one helper. The rest of us waited in a landrover where we could see the area which the net would cover. It was arranged so that the bulldozer spreading the rubbish delivered regularly by lorries would work the area in front of the net to bring the gulls down. But we knew that we might get only one shot and that was going to be difficult. Doctor Watson, firing the net, had to choose a moment as the gulls settled when the iron bars fired by the cannons to carry the net would not kill any birds – he was looking for a momentary gap in the white cloud. The cameraman was going to shoot at higher than normal speed – over-crank the camera that is – to catch the flight of the net in slow motion. He would have a split second to start rolling. In this tense atmosphere we waited, and waited – an

The large numbers of seagulls wintering inland have caused problems: here a 'cannon net' is used to catch a sample for ringing.

hour went by, and we were thinking of calling it off after an hour and a half when the gulls which had been sitting all around the area of the trap suddenly moved in. The cannons fired, and everyone ran. Under the net were about one hundred and fifty seagulls.

One of the first ones lifted carefully out and put into a canvas bag had a ring on its leg from Estonia in Eastern Europe. It was a black-headed gull, and one of a great many of these birds which breed each spring around the Baltic Sea, then move across Europe towards London and its rubbish tips in late summer, to stay until the following spring. Another gull had been ringed when young at its nest site in East Germany. Here, on Rainham rubbish tip, was proof that the great flocks of gulls that winter in England, and congregate around the towns, come from all over north and east Europe. The rings that were put on the unmarked birds that day may end up back in the Baltic, and some are found and recorded so that the movement and the numbers of these gulls can be computed. Most of those we caught were black-headed, with a few common gulls amongst them. On other tips, the lesser black-backed gulls are in the majority – the flocks have their chosen scavenging grounds, and they have fairly fixed flight paths each day between their feeding areas and roosting sites. Those at Rainham mostly go out to the Thames estuary, and are probably not a problem for aircraft or as vectors of disease, though plenty of people complain about them.

At Heathrow airport, the same species is a hazard. It is unfortunate, and a fine example of the way in which man can fool unintentionally with the ecosystem, that airports have been sited on the outskirts of towns, in tracts of land developed to attract large numbers of birds. To the west of Heathrow is a series of enormous reservoirs; right on the edge of the airfield is Perry Oaks sludge treatment works which includes several muddy artificial lakes which are next to a small pond used by the staff angling club. There are gravel pits close by, which, if filled in by rubbish or turned into a lake when extraction is complete, will attract birds. And the airport itself, with great expanses of turf, undisturbed by anything but aeroplanes landing and taking off, is attractive to a good deal of wildlife.

On our first visit to the airport in the winter there were few birds around. One or two herons were hunting around the angling club lake, and a canal which runs down the edge of the sewage works. The herons use the end of one runway as a 'standing' ground after they have fed. We set out across the strange landscape of the airport to find one of the yellow jeeps which patrol constantly with flashing orange lights in an operation known as 'Seagull', looking left and right as we crossed the runways. From ground level, the jumbos look enormous and quite terrifying as they taxi past.

'Operation Seagull' is a critical part of the airport's safety routine. The yellow jeeps are equipped with a broadcast system, and the operators carry a series of cassettes with recordings of the alarm calls of a variety of species including lapwing, black-headed gull, and lesser black-backed gull. The two-man crews have to be able to identify the species they are dealing with if they are going to have any chance of clearing a flock which has settled in a potentially dangerous position. They first play the alarm call, which with some species is designed to act as a scarifier and with others to attract the flock. If distress calls do not work, one of the crew steps out and fires rockets into the air. How effective this is we could not tell, because there were very few birds around. We saw a kestrel chasing a starling into Perry Oaks sewage works, a crow, a

A study of seagulls caught with nets shows that most breed around the Baltic, and some caught here at Rainham were born in Russia.

heron and one or two gulls. It was much the same when we went back to film at Heathrow.

There was other wildlife here, however. Rabbits right next to one of the runways, had burrowed out through the snow and hopped around prettily, leaving comical tracks around the warren. At one time, the rabbits did cause a problem by feeding in front of one of the automatic pilot beams on the ground and throwing the system into confusion, but now they seem to be of little concern. There are foxes here too, which the safety officers watch but do not appear to be too worried about. We were shown a fox's earth right out on the airfield within a few feet of one of the runways: tracks led up to the snow-covered hole in the ground, and away

Rabbits can be troublesome in London, as they are in the countryside. Park-keepers shoot them, and they have caused problems at Heathrow Airport.

again, and as we followed these jets roared into the sky above our heads.

The most difficult time of the year for 'Operation Seagull' is in late summer when the gulls return in large numbers from their breeding grounds. In recent years, flocks have taken to arriving after dark, and roosting in the deserted parking bays of Heathrow. They are not a problem there, but if they all take off at once in the morning, or if startled at night – perhaps by the foxes which often prey on roosting birds – they could bring a plane down.

Fortunately there are very few serious accidents caused by collisions between birds and aeroplanes, but the *potential* for disaster is frightening. Here are one or two figures. In Europe, between 1976 and 1980, there were well over 7,000 incidents of bird-strikes: Switzerland had the highest figures, and the UK about average, with 4.3 strikes for every 10,000 aircraft 'movements'. Of incidents where the species of bird involved could be identified, nearly half involved seagulls of one kind or another. Heathrow had a total of just over 200 strikes in this period, but, given the very large traffic there, quite a low rate of 2.1 per 10,000 movements.

Many of the birds involved are quite small: swallows, martins, starlings but most of them, like the gulls weigh about one pound. If these small birds are involved, they are not usually large enough to bring an aircraft down. An analysis of which bits of an aircraft get hit most often showed that about a third of strikes were to the nose, and fifteen per cent to the windscreen. Landing gear was hit in five per cent of the cases; engines in sixteen; the wing in fourteen per cent; the fuselage in seventeen and the tailplane in one per cent.

Although very few accidents are fatal, the damage caused to aircraft is often severe: an estimate is that, in Europe, bird strikes cost about 17 million dollars between 1976 and 1980. So

'Operation Seagull' is taken seriously, and the Civil Aviation Authority requires all airport operators to take measures to control bird movements.

To know how to control the birds, you have to know something about their behaviour and ecology, and ornithological experts have been consulted on many occasions on the best ways to handle the problem. At Royal Air Force aerodromes, birds of prey flown by falconers have been used to clear the area before take-off. But a more effective technique employing a kind of 'eco-control' has been developed at airports: to grow the grass longer. This is quite a difficult task, for the grass has to be long enough to deter gulls and other birds from settling on it – they don't like to feed in turf which is taller than they are – but not so long that it obscures lights, and makes it difficult for rescue and other vehicles to cross the airport. The recommended height is six to eight inches, and this can only be achieved with careful management. In some places, a local farmer has taken over the land and cuts the grass for hay. Weeds have to be kept out of it as far as possible because their seeds attract wood pigeons and other birds.

What would happen if the rabbits began to graze the grass on a large scale so that it was kept short, we do not know; perhaps Heathrow could encourage the foxes. Another possibility is that the long grass will attract small mammals, voles and fieldmice, and this will bring in the birds of prey. There are already kestrels around Heathrow, and on the Perry Oaks sludge works short-eared owls are not uncommon winter visitors.

The other major effort in keeping troublesome wildlife away from airports has been an attempt to ensure that rubbish dumps are not sited near them and that gravel pits, when they are exhausted, are not developed in a way which will attract gulls and other birds. During this century, the handling of London's ever increasing mounds of rubbish has evolved so that small local tips are closed down, and the bulk of it is shipped to the outskirts of town where it is dumped on massive land-fill sites well away from the city. The one we filmed at Rainham, is by the Thames, and was first used at the beginning of the century. Rubbish is loaded into barges in central London, and then pulled by tugs down to Rainham, where it is transferred to lorries which take it out into the great wasteland of the tip. Around the dock area, are nets put up to trap the rubbish that is caught in the wind. This makes an eerie sight, reminiscent of a fishing port, with the gulls in large flocks overhead, wheeling down to settle on the barges as they come in or to grab scraps from the lorries.

To prevent the rubbish blowing away and to make it less accessible to foxes, rats, cats, gulls and other birds, it is covered each day in a layer of earth. In time, the earth is colonised by plants, one of the most common of which is hemlock – the source of one of the deadliest poisons. Many other weed species get established, forming a kind of rubbish-based savannah, which has attracted an interesting variety of birds, like the stonechat. Most surprising are the skylarks, which not only winter here, but nest too, rising with their trilling song above the overgrown rubble, while lorries rumble out to the working part of the site. Skylarks were one species of bird which could not recolonise the town when suburbia was built over the meadows they used to inhabit, but the refuse disposal system has provided them with a new landscape in which to live.

By covering the rubbish tips with earth, life has been made more difficult for the scavengers, but in time has produced a place for other species: the

ecological effects of any kind of 'progress' are always complex. Recent attempts have been made to tidy the tips up even more by bringing rubbish down river in containers, and taking it covered over to the tip, so the seagulls may have a harder time of it in future. However, the gulls are now so well established in Europe and have found so many feeding grounds from playing fields to St James's Park, that neater rubbish tips will not get rid of them. There is a clear conflict between man and wildlife in the case of the rubbish tips, the reservoirs, the gulls and the airports. But there have been other changes this century in which you might imagine the interests of man and of wildlife are more or less identical. The most dramatic of these has been the cleaning up of the Thames.

It was the invention of the water closet in the early nineteenth century which began the deterioration of the Thames – an early example of the advance of progress having disastrous ecological repercussions. Before the water closet came along, sewage in the capital was collected in cesspits below houses. These were emptied from time to time by night soil men, who had the revolting job of fishing it out in buckets and trundling it out to the market gardens around London to be used as fertiliser. The closet needed a flushing system, and the first inefficient sewers were built, pouring effluent straight into the river, which right up to the middle of the century was both a sewer and a source of water supply.

The river was not exactly clean in the eighteenth century, as it was used to swill the offal from the many slaughter-houses in London down-river, but the discharge of sewage from a rapidly rising population had by the 1830s begun to have serious effects on the life of the river.

For centuries, the Thames had provided a rich fishing ground and sup-

The seagulls wheeling above the Thames at Rainham are more interested in London's rubbish than the fish in the river.

ported a very lively industry all the way from the estuary to the upper reaches. It is a tidal river right through London, and the mix of fresh and salt water varies according to the run of the tide and the flow of rain-water upstream. Nearer the sea, are the salt-water fish, and furthest away are the freshwater fish. In between, a number of species, such as the flounder, which can live in both fresh and salt water, thrived. The tides shunt water up and down the river (if you drop a piece of timber off London Bridge it is sent back and forwards and might take 40 days to get to the sea). The Thames was a river very rich in food, but it has always been vulnerable to pollution because of this swilling backwards and forwards. It was never a really great salmon river, and the salmon was one of the first fish to disappear. Up to the turn of the

century, plenty were caught: 1801 was a bumper year with sixty-six fish taken at Boulter's lock, weighing more than a total of 1,000 pounds. From then on, the salmon went into decline, and, by 1830, they seem to have disappeared altogether upstream of London. Even in 1821, the offer of thirty shillings a pound for a Thames salmon to celebrate the coronation of King George IV produced no fish at all.

The disappearance of the salmon was not entirely due to pollution. Its spawning grounds, and its chances of reaching them, were badly affected by the building of weirs, such as that at Teddington in 1811, and the construction of locks to improve navigation on the river. Both had the effect of destroying shallow spawning grounds, deepening the river, and providing traps in which the congregating salmon

A sample of both sea and fresh water fish caught in the filters at West Thurrock power station.

could easily be taken. Even without these problems the salmon would have had difficulty surviving beyond the middle of the century, for untreated sewage in water produces a growth of bacteria which absorbs oxygen, and salmon need a high level of dissolved oxygen to live.

Other fish survived longer, but the whole of the Thames fishing industry was in decline by the 1860s. By then, the stench of the river had become so bad that Parliament finally voted the money to do something about it, and the massive sewage systems which are still in use today, were built north and south of the river by the Metropolitan Board of Works, the first London-wide local authority set up for that purpose. Sewage was carried out to the east, and was pumped into the river at Barking on the north bank and Crossness on the south. This shifted the problem downstream. Later, solid matter was separated out and taken out to sea, so that the accumulation of sewage was not as bad at the river outfalls.

The river did begin to revive and there were unsuccessful attempts to reintroduce the salmon from 1901. Fishing as a sport continued on the river, and in the dock pools which were cut off from the mainstream and therefore partly protected from pollution. But from this time on, the river got steadily worse. The growth of semi-detached London outstripped the provision of effective sewage works, and more effluent was pumped into the river. Industrial pollution from gas and chemical works made things worse. The bombing in the Second World War destroyed many sewage pipes, and after the war, new detergents fouled up the system and added a new dimension to the pollution.

In 1957, the state of the river had reached an all time low. It was in that year that the London Natural History Society asked Alwynne Wheeler from the Natural History Museum to survey the fish of the tidal Thames. His broad conclusion was that there were no established populations from Kew Bridge to Gravesend, and forty-three miles of the river were mostly devoid of fish except for times in the year when there was a strong flow of water from up-river or temperatures were very low.

Not all wildlife had done badly out of this sorry state of affairs. In the mud of the river bed, a couple of species of a little red worm called the tubifex had thrived in polluted water, and were there in such abundance that they provided a living for people who collected them and sold them as aquarium food, for both fish and birds love to eat them. The inefficient sewage works which were a cause of much of the problem, had by then become meccas for bird watchers, for the open sludge beds bred a crawling mass of insects which attracted many insect feeders and wading birds, particularly in the winter. And, of course, the brown rat did very well in the sewers. The lack of oxygen in the river also kept down such troublesome creatures as the barnacle, so in some respects, the boatmen on the river were less troubled by natural 'pests'.

The river water had also been harnessed in a new way, from early in the century, with the arrival of electricity. Before the 1950s, there was no effective national grid which could distribute electricity generated in one area to other parts of the country, so power stations were localised. As part of the process of generation, power stations have to be cooled, and the most readily available agent for this in London was Thames water – the alternative was massive cooling towers. Power stations were built along the river, the most famous at Battersea in 1929. The polluted water did give the power stations some trouble, for algae formed on the inside of the pipes and blocked them, but a river free from wildlife was quite convenient. The power stations drew off cold water, and pumped heated water back into the river, raising the temperature and reducing the amount of oxygen in the water, though the churning effect somewhat compensated for this by mixing the water with air.

The power stations had some effect on the pollution of the river, but they had a more remarkable role to play once the campaign to clean the Thames got underway. In one of the most successful of all conservation projects anywhere in the world, life was returned to the river by a series of improvements to sewage treatment plants and through control of industrial pollution. The first sign that the efforts of the London County Council (as it was then) and the Port of London Authority to clean up the river were successful,

came in March 1964, when a fish appeared in the filter screens of West Thurrock power station, sited on the Thames to the east of London. The filters are revolving screens which remove the debris and solid matter from the water before it is used for cooling in the power station. West Thurrock was being built at the time, and the fish caught the eye of an engineer who took it to Alwynne Wheeler at the Natural History Museum for identification. The fish turned out to be a rare member of the cod family, a lesser fork-beard or tadpole fish. The engineer, a Mr Colman, continued to collect any specimens he saw, and over the next two years more tadpole fish, lampreys, stickleback, a John Dory and a smelt turned up.

Smelt, which are related to the salmon, and migrate within the river estuary, were once caught in large

The return of fish to the Thames was monitored by collecting specimens which were pumped into power stations. West Thurrock is the only one operating near London now.

numbers in the Thames and were of commercial value, so their reappearance was a sign that something important was happening. In 1966 there were other reports of fish turning up in the filter systems of power stations, notably at Fulham, inside the built-up area of London where roach were appearing. This gave Alwynne Wheeler the idea of using a series of power stations along the Thames to collect samples of fish and to monitor the return of the fish, and an arrangement was made for the collection of samples all along the river from Fulham to West Thurrock, including the power station at the Ford motor works at Dagenham.

The successor to the LCC, the Greater London Council, organised fishing competitions on the Thames to provide further evidence of what species were recolonising the river. Between 1967 and 1973, sixty-eight species of fish were collected from the power station filter screens, and another four species were captured in different ways. Of these, eighteen were freshwater fish, such as roach and bream, forty-three were sea-fish such as Dover sole, and eleven were euryhaline – that is, they can live in both fresh and sea water.

Today, more than one hundred species of fish have been recorded in the tidal Thames, and it is teaming with life again. There are salmon in the river, and attempts have been made to get them re-established by introducing young fish to the upper reaches in the hope that they will return to spawn after they have moved down the river and spent some years at sea. It is unlikely, for the reasons given earlier, about the destruction of spawning grounds, that salmon will ever do very well in the Thames, but the fact that they are there at all, and move right through the centre of London is proof of the cleanliness of the river. Further proof is the fact that the eel fisheries have returned and catches from any-

where in the centre of London are considered fit for human consumption.

It is a very strange sight to watch the filter screens at a power station and to see, from time to time, a fish appear, often still in good condition and flapping about. All the stations in inner London have now been closed down, so we had to go to West Thurrock down river to watch the screens in action. The water here is salty, so most species were either sea fish, such as Dover sole and bass, or those which live in either fresh or salt water. However, an enormous bream turned up, as well as a roach and two small perch. There were plenty of smelt, a pretty little fish with a light torquoise tint, which when fresh, smells exactly like cucumber.

All the fish, other than those which

There are sometimes so many fish and other creatures pumped into power stations that they can block the filter screens.

More than one hundred species of fish have now returned to the Thames since better sewage systems have made the water cleaner.

had been injured in some way as they were sucked into the power station and on to the screens, looked in good condition, and just to prove that the river really was clean we asked Alwynne Wheeler and David Rickard from the Thames Water Authority to eat some. We grilled some smelt on a charcoal stove, and they were delicious. Because of the concern about the welfare of fish accidentally sucked into the power station, an outflow has been built so that those which pass through the screens still alive can swim back into the river via a small stream. When the tide is out this runs through the estuarine mud, and attracts seagulls and herons which have discovered a very handy source of food. We also saw people with buckets collecting fish at the outflow, and were told – though we

were not able to check – that they were gypsies who had established a small trade selling power station fish in the market.

While Alwynne Wheeler was doing his research in to the return of fish to the Thames, he often visited the power stations, and lost prize specimens to gulls which would snatch them from the top of the screens, or to the station cats which were adept at hooking them off with a paw. At West Thurrock they have had to protect the top of the screens with wire mesh because in the winter so many herons were congregating to catch fish there. Some herons lost their footing and were sucked down to their death. But the station staff were also uneasy about forty of these very large birds with enormous terrifying beaks hanging around the screens.

Grey herons wait for fish to be pumped back into the Thames after passing through the filter system at West Thurrock.

So wildlife quickly began to become a problem for the power stations as the river became cleaner. Mussels began to grow in the labyrinth of water pipes at the stations, and the weight of shrimps and shoals of fish at certain times of the year threatens to block the filter screens and to foul the cooling system. Sometimes there is an influx of a small coral-like creature, whiteweed, that looks rather like a plant. This, too, can seriously affect the operation of the power station.

There were other interesting ecological effects as the water became cleaner. At first there was still a great abundance of the tubifex worms which could tolerate the severely polluted water because they take in most of their oxygen direct from the air when the tide is out. When the water was clean enough for freshwater fish to move back into the metropolitan part of the river, bream, which are bottom feeders, did exceptionally well because of this abundant food supply. But as the water got cleaner and the tubifex had to compete with more species in the mud and declined, bream seem to have fallen in number, and surface feeders such as dace are doing better as more insects colonise the upper areas of the water.

In the early 1960s when the return of fish to the Thames was revealed, there was a much more visible influx of wildlife. There appeared on the river, for the first time in living memory, vast flocks of wild duck which looked quite incongruous against the ruined edifices of declining dockland as they moved from their daytime feeding grounds to their evening roosts. In 1968, in one mass were fifteen hundred pochard, a diving duck unknown on the Thames within the London area when the river was serious polluted. There were also shelduck, teal, pintail, tufted duck and mallard. The arrival of large flocks of wild duck was clearly something to do with the river becoming cleaner. When it was severely polluted they could not safely land on the water or mud banks, because of a film of detergent which destroyed the water-proofing of their wings and the oily, stinking hydrogen sulphide gunge. But what were they feeding on? A sample of five species of duck, and a small wader, the dunlin, were shot for research, and the contents of their stomachs examined. Some, like the mallard, were eating the green plants which were returning to the water. But all were, like the bream, feeding extensively on the tubifex worm.

There, are in fact, four species of tubifex in the Thames each with its own requirements in terms of oxygen – which is related to pollution – and its tolerance of salt water. For a few years, before the pollution tolerant species began to decline, there was an exceptional abundance of tubiflex in the mud of the river which were eaten by birds which caught them at low tide – like the dunlin – or up-ended to feed on them in shallow water. At its peak, the Thames around Dagenham became a wintering ground for wildfowl of international importance, with a total number of birds estimated at ten thousand. As the Thames became clearer, the population of wildfowl began to fall away, for their principal food, the tubifex, was in decline. The river remains a good wintering ground for wildfowl and we saw flocks of tufted ducks from our office window, as well as teal. At the outflow of the modernised sewage works at Barking Creek, where the so-called 'high-quality' water flows in to the Thames like a foaming Scottish burn, we saw quite large flocks of cormorant – relatively recent winter visitors to the capital – dunlin, pintail, grebes, a goosander, scaup, pochard, tufted duck, redshank, and a snipe.

The enormous flocks of wildfowl seem to have gone, and in other ways the Thames has become a less hospit-

In winter, the purified outflow from Barking Creek sewage station is a favourite feeding ground for cormorants, wild duck and wading birds.

able place for birds which feed along the muddy banks of the river at low tide. In order to prevent the risk of a disastrous flood in central London, brought on by a combination of heavy rain, high tides and north-easterly winds, a barrier was built. The barrier itself will not often be used, but when it is it will stem the flood of the tide and cause a terrific back swell of water down stream. To prevent flooding below this level the banks have had to be built up. This has taken away some of the feeding grounds of wildfowl. Upstream, the cleaner water has revived the Thames as a pleasure ground, and while commercial traffic has declined, the ferries and motor boats have multiplied, disturbing the river, introducing some pollution from spilt diesel fuel and churning the water which erodes the banks. So the ability of wildlife to take advantage of the cleaner river has been offset by the greater disturbance of people messing about in boats. And, of course, the return of the fish has brought in many more anglers, whose discarded tackle has produced a new hazard for birds.

Nobody would argue that the clean-up of the river has been anything but good, but it has not been a simple case of mutual benefit for wildlife and Londoners – conflicts of interest remain. Most of the wildlife which has been attracted to the river, the fish and the birds, has not been a pest. There was a resurgence of a wood-boring ship worm which did some damage to wooden piers; masses of whiteweed, and brown shrimps have sometimes clogged up the power station at West Thurrock, and the cormorants are becoming a nuisance near the Thames at Walthamstow reservoirs – they have taken on raiding angling club waters stocked with trout.

A great deal of wildlife in towns – whether it colonised them long ago or arrived only recently – is, however, regarded as an out-and-out pest. All local authorities still have pest control officers of some kind, and there is thriving business founded solely on the desire to rid homes, warehouses, hospitals, factories and other places of wildlife which, one way or another, is a nuisance or a serious health hazard. After leafing through a few wildlife books, with glossy photographs of birds, mammals and insects, it is quite a shock to pick up a brochure produced by a pest control firm, such as Rentokil. Here are some of the same species presented in quite a different light, and captioned in such a way as to strike terror into our hearts: beware of the gull, the starling, the pigeon, the cockroach, the rat, the mouse, and the pharoah's ant.

It is precisely the same sensation that you get when you put down a book of British wildflowers, and pick one up on agricultural weeds. Exactly the same species is transformed from a beautiful and interesting plant into a villain. In the Rentokil brochure, in which white-coated people are seen spraying, shooting and trapping, are pictures of pigeons or starlings nests which have blocked gutters and drains: gulls which are raiding grain stores, mice gnawing away at the kitchen dresser. In the town, as in the countryside, there is a great deal of unwanted wildlife.

One of the oddest of autumnal scenes in London we experienced was standing in Leicester Square in the early evening as the flocks of roosting starlings tumbled down through the neon glow of the cinema lights to settle on the plane trees and ledges of buildings. As they did so, a park-keeper was turning over the benches in the square, and a strange sound emanated from high up on the trees, piercing the loud clattering of the birds. A starling alarm call was being broadcast in an effort to frighten the birds away, but the park-keeper was not banking on this control method

Enormous flocks of starlings like these gathering in Whitehall before roosting on Duck Island in St James's Park have caused problems.

working, and he was protecting the seats of the benches from a nightly covering of bird lime. In the countryside, very large starling roosts can kill off woodland so much lime is deposited on the branches and the ground, for starlings return to the same place each evening. In London, the problem is that in a single evening anything – a bench, or a bicycle or a car – left under a starling roost will have a very nasty layer of guano on it in the morning.

The starlings create a special hazard because their roosts are so large, but nobody yet has found a satisfactory way of shifting them. Buildings can be coated with a substance which discourage the birds from landing, and this does seem to be locally successful, but the roost shifts around, moving from trees to buildings, as the leaves fall in late autumn, and moving from place to place in the winter.

London pigeons do not have such large roosts as the starlings, but then they hang around in the centre of town all day, and live in colonies which stick to the same territories unless they are disturbed. They, too, deposit tons of guano on buildings and statues, eroding the stonework and creating an unsightly and sometimes unhealthy mess. Pigeon colonies nest either in the eves of buildings, on ledges or in lofts, and in time a thick layer of droppings, nest material, broken eggs, and dead birds builds up and become infested with all kinds of parasites. In the past, the strange noises from these free range dove-cotes in the attics of buildings have been the origin of ghost stories as well and have allegedly driven terrified owners to abandon the buildings!

The economic cost of cleaning up after the pigeons, starlings, and other species such as sparrows and gulls which add their own splashes of white to the heads of distinguished stone figures, such as Lord Nelson, is quite considerable. Westminster City Council spend no less than £50,000 each year on cleaning up after these birds, and Trafalgar Square is washed every day and the fountain water replaced every three weeks to remove bird droppings and other waste.

Occasional attempts are made to reduce the pigeon population, by trapping, shooting, and poisoning, but such is the ambivalent attitude towards wildlife in the city that the job of pest control officers is difficult. You cannot turn out in the early morning with a rifle to shoot pigeons in the centre of London without being set upon by an angry crowd, and pigeons are frequently released from traps by animal lovers. And it is impossible to get rid of a bird like the pigeon if its numbers are kept artificially high by a benevolent public that provides them with a limitless supply of food. If you ban the feeding of pigeons in one place, they will shift to another.

Pest species are, by their very nature, extremely successful inhabitants of towns, the brown rat which lives in the sewers being an excellent example. Its success is largely a result of the sewage system, for this is a ground living species, which likes to be near water and is a good swimmer. It emerges from the sewers to raid rubbish tips, dustbins and warehouses, but is no longer common – as it was in the Victorian slums – in houses. It breeds at such a pace that it has already produced strains resistant to such poisons as warfarin.

The brown rat is thought to be a native of Asia, from where it spread along the trade and shipping routes to Europe, arriving in England around 1728. At that time, there was already resident the black rat (with the nice Latin name of *Rattus rattus*), which was probably introduced centuries earlier from South East Asia. It was the black rat that carried the fleas which caused the plagues. The brown rat has gradually replaced the black rat, though

The fouling of buildings and monuments by pigeons and other birds presents Westminster Council with an enormous cleaning bill.

The brown rat, which like much urban wildlife is considered a pest, thrives in the dirtiest parts of town.

whether or not it was the result of direct competition is not clear. The black rat is really a tree rat, and it lives in the tops of buildings, inhabiting a different layer in the man-made environment of the town from the brown rat.

The black rat is still about in London, but, as we discovered when we went in search of one to film it is very rare. Rentokil had one at their laboratories in East Grinstead, but it was a very old and mangey specimen which, in a trial run, refused to move at all at first. Then, suddenly, it shot straight up the wall as if there were nothing there and perched on a metal pipe. Black rats are extraordinarily good climbers, much better than brown rats, but it seems that modern buildings do not suit them and they are an endangered species surviving in only a few areas. The brown rat is doing very well.

Generally speaking, the filthier a town is, the better the many pest species such as rats and mice will do. Whole host of cockroaches, many of them introduced accidently from abroad, thrive in unhygienic kitchens and buildings. Some well established pest species have been inadvertently foiled by new inventions, such as the advent of synthetic garments which cannot be eaten by the larvae of cloths moths, or the widespread installation of central heating which has reduced the incidence of a spider called *Pholus phalangioides* which needs a certain amount of moisture to survive. It is the kind which hangs from threads in the corners of rooms, so the cobweb must be

Housemice are probably less common than they once were in houses, but they can be found everywhere in London and are often seen on Underground stations.

less common problem in spring cleaning than it was.

While central heating may have driven some creatures out, it has allowed others in. One of these is the pharoah's ant, a native of the tropics, which first made its way to Britain, by boat no doubt, in 1828. At first it probably survived in greenhouses, for it cannot live through an English winter out of doors, and by 1900 it had become a serious pest. Its odd name arises from the belief that it was responsible for one of the legendary plagues of Egypt. Whether or not this is true, it has certainly become one of the most dangerous and widespread pests in London and other southern towns. The pharoah's ant is tiny, only two millimetres long, and much smaller than the familiar black garden ant. In one crucial respect it behaves very differently from the black ant. Whereas the garden ant, which can be a nuisance in kitchens, establishes a fixed nest, the pharoah's ant does not. It is in hospitals that these ants have become a special menace. They require a great deal of moisture which means that they congregate in insanitary areas such as toilets. They then travel about in search of food. There are some quite horrific stories of hospital infestations, for pharoah's ants, being tiny, can get into bandages and feed on supporating wounds, with a risk of infection. They have been found in babies' incubators and biting babies' eyelids. It seems they are also attracted to patients with high fevers.

Pharoah's ants can also spread infections on housing estates, and if they become established in tower blocks, among the labyrinth of ducts and pipes are very difficult to eliminate. There is a story of them feeding in the eczema sores of a young girl asleep in bed in her home in Barnet. These ants have caused problems which require drastic action. Whole blocks of flats have been evacuated to allow pest control teams to go in with pesticides and poisons. For a time hospitals have been closed down too, because their ants have got into equipment and dressings and effectively wrecked the sterile areas. So far, these ants have been found to carry up to twenty kinds of potentially dangerous bacteria. Pharoah's ants can spread quickly because a group of workers will take eggs from an original nest, containing a new queen, and carry them to another site where a new, satellite colony is established. An effective bait has been found, administered on raw liver left for the workers to carry back to their nests, but it can take weeks or months to clear a large hospital or tower block.

So here is another example of 'progress' and improvement in living conditions, attracting unwelcome wildlife. It would be possible to list a great many other living things which are not wanted in town – dry rot for example – but the essential point should be obvious. You cannot argue that the interests of man and wildlife are identical, unless you rule out all those species that at one time or another become a nuisance or a serious pest. There would be disagreement, anyway, about what was really a pest and what was not. Is the urban fox, for example, to be welcomed? It is a great thrill for many people to discover that their suburban garden has attracted foxes, as if this were the final consummation of their efforts to create a little bit of rural England in suburbia. Yet their next door neighbours will call in the pest control officers to get rid of the foxes. This ambivalent attitude has become the subject of a now very popular, and no doubt apocryphal, story of politicians. We first heard the story as set in Glasgow. The member of parliament is listening to complaints from residents on a council estate. Rats, they say, are the problem, and a promise is made to

Shags on Hungerford Bridge.

bring in pest control. Then someone stands up and says, 'It's the foxes too.' They debate what to do, aware that the eco-lobby might not like it if they harm the foxes. It is suggested that if the foxes have to go they should be exterminated humanely, by gassing. Everyone agrees: 'Aye, gas the foxes'. Later, at a meeting with council officials, the police, environmental health and social workers, the proposal is put forward. There is a silence, then a social worker tells them: 'The Foxes are a family who live on the estate.'

The red fox is already being woven into urban folklore, just as it became part of folklore in the countryside, where the conflicts between the interests of man and of wildlife, have always been recognised. It is quite likely, as more species become established in the city, the conflicts will not diminish but grow and that the romantic view of an entirely benign community of wild creatures living in town will be seen for what it is: wishful thinking.

People will continue to pick and choose the wildlife they want around us, as they have always done. However, as a greater interest in natural history spreads, it may well be that when conflicts arise they will be prepared to give much greater scope to wildlife than they have done in the past.

As commuters head home over Waterloo Bridge, many birds, including thousands of starlings, head into London to roost.

A wild area in Battersea Park where flowers like hawksbeard escape the gardener's hoe.

EPILOGUE

ONE OF THE effects of spending a long time tracking down wildlife in the city and trying to understand how it survives there was to give us a novel, animal's-eye-view of the urban landscape. We found ourselves assessing famous buildings such as St Paul's Cathedral or Westminster Abbey not as architectural masterpieces, but as potential nest-sites for kestrels or house martins. We would contemplate a well-landscaped park or garden not as a vista pleasing to the human eye, but more prosaically as a habitat which might limit the activities of voles or nesting warblers.

We began to treat the whole of the town not as the enormous human artefact that it is, but as a rocky region of the country cut through with canyons which roared to the sound of traffic. The canals and reservoirs, parks and gardens were oases or islands which wildlife might try to reach from the countryside, having crossed the great savannah of suburban gardens which form the outer fringes of the capital.

A wide variety of wildlife had managed to colonise the archipelego of urban islands, and some species had arrived only recently: the magpie, the fox, the long-tailed tit and so on. An understanding of how and why this had happened involved a very complicated line of investigation. How did individual species behave? What did they need in the way of food at different times of the year, how large a territory did they hold, were they essentially gregarious or solitary? Then, what did

the town have to offer in the way of trees, insect food, undisturbed areas, shrubs. We realised, too, that the town could not be treated in isolation. Much of this wildlife was expanding its range from countryside to town, so we needed to know what its history was in rural areas – was it recovering from persecution by gamekeepers, or had its numbers risen because a change in agricultural practice had favoured it?

It was rather like a *City Safari* board game, the aim of which was to discover which species would make it into town across a series of obstacles, with a few ladders as well as snakes. We could imagine a pack of cards which represented advantages and set-backs for particular kinds of wildlife. 'Royal Parks fell all old trees – bats and woodpeckers go back ten paces.' Or 'Conservationists create ten new ponds in central London – frogs, toads and newts advance ten paces.' In many cases, events hundreds or thousands of miles away would influence the success of certain species. 'Drought spreads in Sahara – house martins lose three nesting colonies in central London.' The aim of the game would be to work out just how much wildlife you could, with the most favourable circumstances, cram into an area within a two-mile radius of Charing Cross.

There is now in London, and other major cities in Britain, Europe and North America, a group of urban ecologists or conservationists who are playing this game for real. Whereas in the past only a handful of naturalists considered the town as an appropriate place for wildlife, the urban landscape is now regarded as a region with immense potential value. Exactly the same kind of conservationist principles that are used to defend the last remaining wildernesses of Africa can be applied to bits of overgrown railway land in London, to reservoirs and even to the Royal Parks.

Just as a great deal of wildlife has colonised the town, so too, in recent years have many ecologists who regard its artificial landscape as a potentially valuable part of Planet Earth. Members of the recently formed London Wildlife Trust, or the older Flora and Fauna Preservation Society can be found engaged on Wimbledon Common, Hampstead Heath or in Hyde Park in what we came to call 'eco-gardening'.

They fell trees so that ponds which have filled up with leaf litter can once again become breeding grounds for frogs or toads; they chop down non-native shrubs like rhododendron bushes so that native species can reassert themselves; they argue with park-keepers and groundsmen to persuade them to let grass grow longer and to leave important food plants for insects – nettles, for example, which are essential for some butterflies such as the peacock.

In many instances, these conservationists find themselves in conflict with other interests in the city – all land is so valuable, and has so many alternative uses for sport, or housing or industry that the eco-lobby in town has to fight as many battles as its counterparts in the countryside who attempt to save woodland or hedgerows from the bulldozers of the modern farmer.

The conservationists are now there at every public inquiry into the proposed destruction of a piece of woodland in town, or the removal of any open space, adding their voice to the traditional opposition from people who want to preserve these places for their own recreation. Already, the conservationists have won some notable victories with their arguments that even small urban islands of greenery are a haven for a wide range of species – even if most of the creatures are beetles or snails in which few people take an interest. The names of places saved, such as the Gunnersbury Triangle, trip of the tongues of the cognoscenti as if they were Yellowstone Park or the Serengeti rather than six acres of overgrown surplus railway land in West London.

It is this new conservationist movement which has made urban wildlife a political issue, and, indirectly, led to our own exploration of the subject. We found that we could not agree with all the conservationists' claims about the true potential of the town as a wildlife reserve. Some of the ways in which they were trying to attract new species in to town and to increase interest in urban wildlife seemed to be misguided. Around one million pounds was spent buying and planting a small 'natural park' in the shadow of the Victorian gothic mountain range of St Pancras Station. Could the money have been better spent elsewhere?

However, on the essential point that wildlife in the city should not be treated differently from wildlife anywhere else we came to agree wholeheartedly. That was the great revelation of our exploration: the study of urban wildlife is not simply a trivial pursuit of naturalists who happen to find themselves in town. And those creatures which have colonised our cities are not just amusing oddities – they are a proper part of the study of natural history as a whole.

There is a special, spine-tingling kind of drama that goes with the discovery of wildlife in the town, and there was one episode, near the very end of our filming for the television series

A badger enticed into a surburban garden with honey sandwiches.

Autumn gold in Greenwich Park, a beautiful scene, but the leaves are collected and burned so they are of little use to wildlife.

which captured the excitement, and occasional absurdity, of our enterprise. It was a final attempt to film a sequence of the tens of thousands of starlings which descend on Leicester Square to roost on the plane trees in the autumn.

The manager of the Odeon cinema in Leicester Square kindly allowed us on to the roof of the building which has a magnificent view over London. The sun was setting on an almost perfect evening and we could see groups of starlings arriving from the outskirts of London, flying in swarms like bees past Big Ben to gather in Whitehall before their final assault on the Square below us. The gathering of birds goes on for an hour or more, and while we watched, a kestrel slid across the roof tops. It went in amongst a swarm of starlings, which immediately massed in the air and, like a single, black amoeboid being rose and fell above Oxford Street. Later, the kestrel stooped on the Square, then flicked its wings to glide to a perch on Nelson's column.

Later, we tried to film the efforts of Westminster Council to get rid of the starlings – bashing empty dustbins with sticks and playing alarm calls. The noise the council men made had irritated local residents more than the starlings – and in particular had upset the busker who makes a living with performing budgerigars in the Square.

As we tried to interview a council official against the backdrop of the neon lights of the cinemas, the budgie man strode wildy across to us, carrying half a dozen budgies on a stick. The terrible din made to scare the starlings, he yelled, had frightened away one of his star performers. A curious crowd had been drawn by the beating of council drums and strange alarm calls, and lined the railings of the Square. In the glow of our electrician's hand-held lamp they saw this bizarre group of people, and may have heard the busker shout with terrifying passion as he pointed to a timid council official: 'They killed my budgie'.

ACKNOWLEDGEMENTS

WE RECEIVED an enormous amount of help and encouragement in our exploration of urban wildlife, and without the co-operation and collective knowledge of hundreds of people the whole enterprise would have been impossible. Space does not allow us to mention everyone individually, but we would like to express a general thanks to all those who took time to send us information or to show us around their patch of town.

Much of our research was in the parks of London, and we would like to express a special thanks for the wonderful help we were given. The bailiff of the Royal Parks, Ashley Stephenson and all his staff, Jennifer Adams in Hyde Park, Fred Mitchell in St James's Park, Michael Baxter Browne in Richmond Park, David Castleton in Regent's Park, Jim Buttress in Greewich Park and Nick Butler in Kensington Gardens gave us invaluable help. So too did David Smith, the gamekeeper in Richmond Park, who has unrivalled knowledge of the wildlife there and who freely offered his time and expertise. The keen eyed observation of Mike Lewis a park-keeper with a special interest in the birdlife led us to nests we would not otherwise have found. In Regent's Park, the enthusiasm and knowledge of Tony Duckett, the 'birdman' was exceptional.

In the Greater London Council Parks, Geoff Templeman paved the way for the great co-operation we received everywhere, on Hampstead Heath and in Battersea and Trent Park in particular. We are also very grateful to the parks department of Westminster City Council. For the special privilege of being allowed into Buckingham Palace Garden we would like to thank Her Majesty the Queen, and Michael Shea and Sarah Brennan for their great help at what was a difficult time. Without the expertise and enthusiasm of David McClintock our visits to the garden would have been purposeless and much less enjoyable, and we are indebted too to Stanley Cramp, and Fred Kemp for their information and advice. Thanks also to John Bradley of the Natural History Museum for expert advice on the butterflies and moths of the garden. We spent a great deal of time hunting down wildlife in London Zoo, and we owe a special thanks to the long suffering assistance of Joan Crammond, Chief Press Officer. Dave Herbett's personal knowledge of wild birds which have colonised the Zoo and the help he gave us was very valuable. We would also like to thank Brian Bertram and David Moltu for their help on the red squirrel project. For permission to film in their back gardens, a special thanks to Mr and Mrs Cox and Mr and Mrs Woodward.

A great many property owners, companies and authorities helped us by giving access to buildings or industrial sites. The Central Electricity Generating Board made us welcome at West Thurrock power station; Mr Davis arranged for us to watch the Embankment crows from the roof of Electra House. We were given great co-operation by the Thames Water Authority, the London Airports Authority, and Cleanaway Ltd., where Phil Shaw, the resident ecologist, went out of his way to assist us in difficult circumstances. Thanks also to Barry Watson for organising the cannon-netting of seagulls. At Brent reservoir, Peter Creasey gave us superb help, and Ted made us very welcome. Thanks also to Kevin Roberts at Rye Meads Nature reserve and the Selborne Society, the guardians of Perrivale Wood. Peter Bateman of Rentokil Ltd. gave us tremendous help, and thanks also to Adrean Mehan. We are most grateful to the Vintners and Dyers and the Queen's Swan Master. A great many enthusiasts and students of London wildlife gave us their time and expertise. The London Natural History Society provided essential information on changes in urban wildlife, and we would like to thank especially Doug Boyd, John Widgery, and Leo Batten. We are greatly indebted to Tom Langton of the Flora and Fauna Preservation Society for giving us so much assistance with frogs and toads and to Tony Hutson, who advised us on bats. The London Wildlife Trust gave us tremendous support, in particular John Newton, and two member of the habitat survey team David Stubbs and Tony Hare. A special thanks to Eric Simms, for his advice on the birdlife of London and to John Edwards and Roger Beecroft, who gave us valuable advice and assistance. Thanks also to Paul Hillyard who helped us locate numerous spiders. Barry Watson who helped us locate orchids in Thameside and Mike Dennis who introduced us to some spectacular wildlife areas in east London. Frank Schofield saved the day for us and let us film his kestrels' nest in Wembley.

We received great help and co-operation from

the Edward Grey Institute of Field Ornithology, the Nature Conservancy Council and the British Trust for Ornithology. For their help in discussing the themes and ideas of the project we would like to thank Malcolm Coe, Denis Owen and Alwynne Wheeler. Our special thanks to Tim Birkhead whose comments on the text were extremely valuable. Any errors of fact or judgement remain ours.

We would like to thank all our friends and colleagues at London Weekend Television who were involved in the project. A very special thanks to Linda Stradling whose mastery of new technology, constant encouragement and dedication throughout was superb. In the library, Anne Cornell, Mark Noades, Sarah Adair and Mary Murphy made the armchair part of the safari so much easier by their enthusiasm and efficiency in finding often obscure books and texts. Without Jane Hewland, there would have been no *City Safari* project, and we would like to thank also Mike Chaplin, Pat Newbert, Marcelle Ruddell and Beverley Spurdens for their support. Thanks also to Joanna Mack for some very valuable discussions.

Though they were not directly involved in the book we would like to thank the wildlife cameramen Theo Cockerell, Martyn Colbeck and Alistair Macewan who not only shot some remarkable film, but provided us with valuable observations from the field.

We would like to thank Sarah Mahaffy and Carey Smith for their help in the production of the book. Finally a special thanks to Caroline Aitzetmuller for the hours she spent sorting out all the photographs for the book, and to Joyce Moseley for tolerating the domestic disruptions of authorship.

Our sincere gratitude to Olympus Cameras and Kodak Films for their help with equipment and film.

Some of the most attractive species found in London: the dunnock (above) and the robin (below).

Tortoiseshell butterflies (above) and the song thrush (below).

BIBLIOGRAPHY

THERE ARE very few authorative books on wildlife in towns, and Richard Fitter's *London's Natural History* (Collins, 1945) remains one of the best, though it was written 40 years ago, long before ecology and urban conservation became fashionable. The same author's *London's Birds* (Collins, 1949) is also a classic in this field. A much less comprehensive, though more contemporary, survey can be found in John A. Burton's *The Naturalist in London* (David and Charles, 1974). Another relatively recent work which helped create interest in urban wildlife is Richard Maybey's *The Unofficial Countryside* (Collins, 1973). An invaluable reference book for ornothologists is David Montier's *Atlas of Breeding Birds in the London Area* (Batsford, 1977), and for botanists who know their Linnaean Latin (no colloquial plant names are given), there is the *Flora of the London Area* by Rodney Burton (London Natural History Society, 1983). Alwynne Wheeler's *The Tidal Thames* (Routledge, Kegan and Paul, 1979) is an excellent history of the river's decline and revival and P. Grant and J. Harrison's *The Thames Transformed* (Andre Deutsch, 1976) provides useful additional information. Sadly, David McClintock's monograph on the wildlife of Buckingham Palace has never been printed commercially.

Among the historic works, W. H. Hudson's *London Birds* (Longmans Green, 1898) is a classic, and some flowery references to 19th century urban wildlife are included in Richard Jefferies recently reprinted works, such as *Nature Near London* (John Clare Books, 1980) and *The Open Air* (Wildwood House, 1981).

The academic establishment has taken little serious interest in urban wildlife, though many species which are successful in towns have been studied in great detail individually. *The Public Life of the Street Pigeon* (Hutchinson, 1979) by Eric Simms is a comprehensive account of one familiar bird, and J. D. Summer-Smith's *The House Sparrow* (New Naturalist Series, 1967) is another. *Man and Birds* by R. K. Murton (Collins, 1971) inclues quite a bit of information on birds in towns. *The Ecology of Invasions* (Methuen, 1958) is a stimulating book by C. S. Elton, the father of ecology. Although it is not concerned only with urban species, W. S. Bristow's *Spiders* (Collins, 1958) is a very readable classic, and for more detailed identification the recent book by M. Roberts *Spiders of Great Britain and Ireland* (Harley Books, 1985) is invaluable. In an amusingly illustrated series of books there is *Hedgehogs* by Pat Morris and *Frogs and Toads* by Trevor Beebee (Whittet books, 1983 and 1985), both informative and lively. On wasteland plants there is E. J. Salisbury's book *Weeds and Aliens* (Collins, 1961). For really detailed research on animal behaviour it is necessary to go to academic texts such as *Avian Ecology* by C. M. Perrins and T. R. Birkhead (Blackie, 1984).

There has been much more interest in the eco-systems of tropical rain-forests than that of London or other towns, and there really is no definitive work on the subject. However, Dennis Owen's book *Towns and Gardens* in the Rainbird series on the Natural History of Britain and Northern Europe (1978) is useful, and the same author's *What is Ecology?* (Oxford University Press, 1974) is a lively introduction to the subject in general. To follow up the theories of island biogeography which can be loosely applied to London, there are many academic works, which include *Biogeography: An Ecological and Evolutionary Approach* by C. B. Cox and P. D. Moore (Blackwell Scientific Publications, 4th edition, 1985).

INDEX

Andrew Preater 6B